How To Raise Children Without Breaking Your Back

by
Alex Pirie and Hollis Herman, M.S., P.T., OCS

A body manual for new mothers
and the parents of small children

• IBIS Publications •

How To Raise Children Without Breaking Your Back

For Information contact: HealthyWomen Resources
675 Massachusetts Ave, 10th Floor, Cambridge, MA 02139

SECOND EDITION
SECOND PRINTING

About This Book

Our Goal

New babies and the changes that they make in your emotional and physical life require extra time and energy just when it seems like you have less time and less energy than ever before. When you combine the 'more demands' and the 'less time and energy,' you come up with a greater risk for physical problems. For new mothers the stresses of pregnancy and labor only increase the risk.

This is a book to help you with the physical part of parenting. We want to give you practical, concrete support in the form of good information, exercises, stretches, and tips for raising your children without breaking your back (or anything else). Much of what you learn here will be of lifelong value.

We wrote this for new parents, people who are busy above and beyond the call of duty. Nobody is more important to a society than those who take responsibility for its future. Thank you for all the work you've done and all that you will do.

Who We Are

Hollis Herman, M.S., P.T. OCS: The parent of one and a nationally respected and published specialist, consultant, and teacher in the field of women's physical therapy. She is the Co-director of the Maternal and Child Health Center in Cambridge, MA, and Clinical Instructor at the Women's Physical Therapy Center of Braintree Hospital in Weymouth, MA. She specializes in gynecological physical therapy for pre- and post-partum mothers, incontinence and ergonomic education, and cesarean section rehabilitation. She has also done extensive work with older women.

Alex Pirie: A family day care provider and parent of three. He has taught young children (and their parents) for twenty-five years and has written, illustrated, and edited curriculum materials of many kinds. While he was a physical therapy patient of Hollis' (for Thoracic Outlet Syndrome, see page 117), they began to work out safe ways to lift and carry children and to explore practical stretches and exercises for tired, harried parents like themselves. He thought it would be a great idea to expand and share what they had worked out, and their sessions slowly grew into this book.

IBIS Publications: IBIS Publications is a small publisher committed to supporting parents and children through the communication of useful information. We can't answer individual health inquiries or make medical referrals, but we would like to hear from you. To comment on this book, suggest new ideas, share useful resources, or helpful information, please write to us at:

IBIS Publications, P.O. Box 44-1474, W. Somerville, MA 02144

How to Use This Book

Where to Begin

Just about anywhere! This is not a front to back book. You can see in the table of contents that there are four main sections; Birth, Managing Day to Day, Common Problems, and Healing. You can start with a particular problem, a troublesome task, or whatever catches your attention. Begin with what concerns you right now.

Birth: These chapters deal with immediate post-partum problems.

Managing Day to Day: Tips, safe strategies, and stretches for daily activities.

Common Problems: The physical problems most encountered by new parents.

Healing: How to recover from injuries; everything from first aid to physicians.

Lifting and feeding are two things you'll be doing a lot. Both of these tasks have special risks for new parents. Lifting because it's extra hard work and we tend not to be careful about how we lift, and feeding because it means staying in one position for a long time. Special sections about lifting and feeding are included in each of the common problem chapters.

If you wish to know a little more about your anatomy, there is a 'Look Inside' page at the end of each common problem chapter.

The Book Will Guide You

Your body is wonderfully complex. Helping and healing one part of you may depend on strengthening or stretching some other place altogether. Wherever this is true, you'll find a note to guide you to the right section of the book.

Resources

No single book or person is going to answer all of your questions. You'll find a listing of resource groups, publications and information centers at the back of the book. Some are for specific problems and some will help you connect with people who will help you in your search for information.

A Page of Basic Information

At the very end is a page of tips. It gives you the basics and lists the five most important exercises and stretches in this book and tells you where to find them.

> **TIP: Throughout the book you will find boxes like this. They contain tips, information, and precautions related to what you're reading.**

Table of Contents

CAUTION: This book is not intended as medical advice. Its purpose is solely informational and educational. Please consult a doctor or other health care professional should the need be indicated for any reason.

Healing From Episiotomies and Tearing

Episiotomies and tearing are the two most common birth injuries for new mothers. Many women heal quickly from these injuries and have no after effects. Women who do have problems often try to ignore them. Don't let this be you. The time right after birth is the best time for healing from a period of great stress. If you are "not feeling right down there," or suspect that your episiotomy or tear has left you with physical problems, it's worth investigating and doing something about it. In almost all cases treatment is simple and effective, and the benefits will be lifelong.

Episiotomies

An episiotomy is a surgical cut in the perineum. Unfortunately, seven out of every ten vaginal births in the United States are accompanied by an episiotomy. As with the cesarean section, this rate far exceeds that of any other similar country.

We all hope this rate will begin to drop. A number of recent medical studies have called into question the usefulness of episiotomies in all but certain special cases. Medical education once justified an episiotomy with statements like "a clean wound heals better than a ragged one," "the baby comes out easier," and "the woman doesn't even feel the cut." The medical literature now states that there is no medical benefit from an episiotomy, except in circumstances such as a forceps delivery. In fact, there is some evidence that episiotomies can contribute to more severe tearing and even greater discomfort for the mother.

Until things change, if you have had a vaginal birth in a hospital, the chances are that you will have had an episiotomy with stitches. You will find this chapter helpful.

Tearing

Tearing of the perineum can occur during vaginal deliveries. Tearing can be just minor tears in the skin, or you can experience more severe tearing which may also include muscle, and, possibly, urethral or anal sphincters. The more severe tears require stitches and a period of discomfort as you heal.

In most cases there are no serious consequences from either episiotomies or tearing. However, if you did not heal easily and are experiencing discomfort, this chapter will help you.

If you did heal easily, but had stitches, this chapter contains useful information about reducing the effects of any scar tissue.

Injury sites

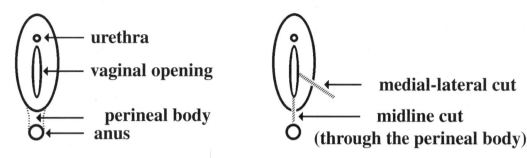

urethra

vaginal opening

perineal body

anus

medial-lateral cut

midline cut
(through the perineal body)

Degrees of Severity

Tearing and episiotomy injuries are classified by their severity. They range from a minor first degree injury to the more serious fourth degree injury. A first degree tear affects only the skin and subcutaneous fat layer. A second degree tear includes damage to the perineal muscles and usually requires stitching. The more severe third degree tear may reach the anal sphincter or toward the clitoris, and the fourth degree tear includes everything mentioned before plus part of the rectal canal. Fourth degree injuries are rare, may require extensive stitching, and may cause fecal incontinence.

An episiotomy is automatically classified as a second degree injury because muscle is cut. Since the cut itself can lead to further tearing, the danger of a third or fourth degree injury is greater with an episiotomy than without.

A tear or episiotomy that requires stitches will leave scar tissue. This scar tissue may cause discomfort and pain. When an injury involves several layers of tissue the scar may bind the layers together as it heals. This is called an adhesion.

Symptoms

Most women won't have adhesions from episiotomy or tears. Those who do will experience some or all of these symptoms:

- pain during intercourse, usually during initial penetration (also called dyspareunia)
- difficulty inserting a diaphragm or cervical cap
- discomfort inserting a tampon or in gynecological exam
- soreness between the vagina and rectum
- discomfort with bowel movements

> **CAUTION:** If you experience any of these symptoms, you should consult with your health care practitioner about treatment.

Immediate Care

Ice packs can reduce the discomfort of swelling and the feeling of pressure and pulling on the tissues during the first few days. The cold reduces the swelling, relieves the feelings of intense pressure, and helps numb the pain. Ice can be applied regularly, perhaps every two hours, seven to ten minutes at a time.

Commercial cold packs that contain a flexible gel are available at most drugstores. You can also fill a rubber surgical glove with water and lay it on the upturned bottom of a small bowl and freeze it. This will give it a useful, rounded shape. A surgical glove filled with ice chips is another way of applying cold. Remember that any source of cold must be separated from your skin by a layer of cloth.

> **CAUTION: Always wrap any cold medium with a towel or cloth. Direct cold can be uncomfortable and dangerous. Since numbness is common in the perineal area after birth, you may not feel the cold application. Ice or a cold pack applied directly to the skin for too long can freeze tissue.**

Subsequent Care

Scar tissue and its tendency to cause muscles and skin to adhere can be dealt with by simple treatments like massage. You can lift and separate healthy muscle tissue and prevent or reduce adhesion. It is also possible to reduce the size and rigidity of the scar itself. You can use this technique on scars that are even ten to twenty years old, but why not begin now?

How To Massage

Within five to ten days the stitches will dissolve. Once this happens, you can begin to massage the tissues between the vagina and anus. Insert your thumb into your vagina while keeping the index finger over the perineal body above the scar. Gently roll the tissue between thumb and finger. Use a warm compress to get started. This will relax the muscles and allow you to touch yourself with less discomfort.

> **TIP: Scar tissue? Anus? Vagina? Stick your thumb in? If you find this embarrassing, read it twice! The muscles in this region are crucial to your health and well being . They support your internal organs, play a role in sexual function, and maintain continence of both bladder and bowel. Learn to touch, look at, move, and think about this part of your body. It will help you heal faster and stay healthier.**

You can massage the scar tissue from an episiotomy or tear in three directions.

With the grain (working along the line of the scar).

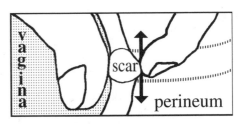

Against the grain (working across the scar).

By rolling the scar between the thumb and forefinger.

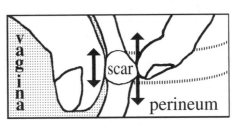

As the scar is massaged it will become smaller, more elastic, and less tender. This permits the tissues of the muscles to regain their function without getting stuck to one another and it reduces the interference of thick masses of scar tissue.

If scar tissue has adhered and is causing discomfort during intercourse, you should have a medical practitioner, either an ob/gyn, a midwife, or a physical therapist specializing in women's health, evaluate your condition. They will help you learn self-massage and will be able to apply deep heating ultrasound to the affected area. (This is not the same ultrasound used to view your baby inside you.) Four or five ultrasound treatments coupled with massage will often make the scarred area painless to the touch and intercourse less uncomfortable.

Pelvic Floor Exercises

An episiotomy or a tear can injure the muscles of the pelvic floor. These muscles form a supporting sling at the bottom of your pelvis. They are vital to the correct positioning and functioning of your internal organs. The next chapter you read in this book should be <u>Strengthening The Pelvic Floor</u> on page 13. It contains exercises that will heal, strengthen, and tone these vital muscles. It's so important that you should read it even if you haven't had any problems at all.

Recovering From Cesarean Sections

A Cesarean Section, or C-section, is a major abdominal surgery performed in special cases to protect the lives of infants and mothers. Unfortunately, it has become a too common part of the American birth experience. In spite of the best efforts of some doctors, medical schools, and childbirth educators, more than one in every five births is a C-section. The operation is so common that it almost seems like a simple and routine procedure. Nothing could be further from the truth. The C-section is major abdominal surgery.

If you have had a Cesarean Section or are a candidate for one, you need extra care and extra attention. Your body will need to recover from a serious operation as well as from the effects of nine months of pregnancy.

The Surgery

A C-section is major surgery. It requires powerful anesthetics and a surgical cut that penetrates through the skin and abdominal muscles into the abdominal cavity and through the uterus itself.

The uterus is the strongest, thickest muscle in the human body. An incision, even along its thinner lower wall is a major physical trauma. It's a tribute to how tough and resilient women are that full healing is possible with proper treatment and care.

The cut may be either up and down along one side of your navel or across the lower belly just above the pubic bone. In either case, once the baby is removed, the uterus, muscles, and other connective tissue are sewn back together and the skin is usually stapled or held together with sterile adhesive strips. This is covered with dressings. The external cut will heal within seven to ten days. The staples or strips are usually removed on the seventh day.

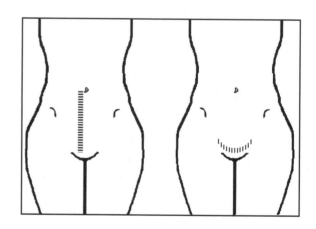

The effects on your abdominal muscles and, sometimes, the nerves serving the muscles of your pelvic floor can persist much longer.

> **TIP: Problems with the muscles of the pelvic floor are not common after a cesarean. However, these muscles are vital for your general health and for future births. Read the pelvic floor chapter (page 13).**

What To Expect

People recover differently from cesareans. You will recover at your own speed. Don't let other people's birth stories confuse you or make you feel badly about the speed of your healing. Instead, listen to your body carefully and respond to its needs. Almost everyone experiences some or all of the problems listed below.

- Pain with coughing or deep breathing.

- Soreness around the incision.

- Severe gas pains.

- Difficulty rolling over and getting out of bed.

- Difficulty straightening up and reaching overhead.

- Pulling sensation in the belly when standing up.

- Pain or difficulty when emptying bowels and bladder.

- Discomfort when nursing from your baby's weight and movement.

You may also experience itching or numbness or both around the incision site. This is because any nerves cut during the operation are beginning to regenerate. Nerve recovery is a slow process and the sensations will probably continue for some time. The scar tissue itself will remain numb.

IMMEDIATE CARE

You can expect excellent post-surgical care from the nursing staff at any hospital that performs cesareans. If you don't get it, demand it. Here are some of the things they should suggest and then help you with.

Move As Soon As Possible

The first, and most important, step in the recovery process is to begin moving by walking around. It helps to have two people supporting you as you begin, one on each side. You may have to push yourself to move through the discomfort. Movement helps prevent fluid settling in your lungs and contributing to a respiratory infection. It also gets your circulation going, starts your muscles healing, and helps keeps your bowel and bladder working well.

Coughing

You should make yourself cough. Try for five good coughs every half hour. This will help clear your lungs and bring in fresh air. It can be painful, but you can reduce discomfort by supporting your stomach. Take a pillow or wadded up sheet or towel and press it firmly over the incision while you cough. This supports your abdomen and reduces the pain as the muscles contract.

Huffing Out

This is a stomach strengthening exercise that you can begin right away. Try saying "HUT!" fast and loudly. It should be as much of a shout as you can manage (bury your face in a pillow if you're worried about disturbing others). You can feel your muscles contract with each exhalation. Do this five times every half hour.

Sucking In

Try pulling your belly in. Start with lower belly (below the navel) and then extend the pull to the area above the navel. Relax and repeat several times, slowly.

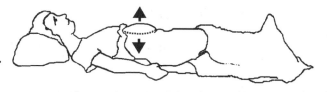

Coordinate your breathing with the in and out movements. Breathe in - imagine your belly filling up with air - and breathe out - imagine your belly sinking down and pushing the air out.

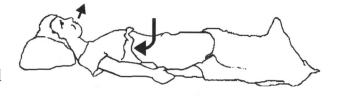

Do this as often as you like, the more often the better. It can be done anywhere, while sitting in a car, nursing, watching TV, reading, or standing.

Getting Support

A Cesarean is major surgery. Don't try to tough things out. Get as much help as you can possibly get while you recover. You'll heal faster and feel better.

Pain Medications

Pain medication can be very helpful. Many are compatible with breastfeeding and will make it easier for you to move around and care for your newborn. Nurses, pharmacists, breastfeeding organizations, professional lactation consultants and doctors can advise you on which drugs will not interfere with breastfeeding.

TENS Units

A very effective device for cesarean rehabilitation is the TENS unit. TENS stands for "Transcutaneous Electrical Nerve Stimulation." These portable, easy to use and easy to conceal devices are smaller than pocket tape players. They give a constant, non-painful stimulus to the abdominal muscles which blocks the sensation of pain.

TENS units can help women to reduce the amounts of pain medication and get out of bed faster, usually within a few hours of the cesarean. (You may not want to get out of bed, but it's important that you do for the reasons mentioned above.). They may enable you to leave the hospital up to one and a half days sooner and have fewer problems with gas pain and flatulence.

Abdominal Binders

Your health care practitioner may recommend an abdominal binder. This is a corset like support that wraps around your middle and acts as a temporary splint for the healing abdominal muscles. Remember that you can begin doing simple exercises as soon as your incision heals and that rapid progress is possible. You can do your exercises while wearing the binder.

SUBSEQUENT CARE

Many things make it difficult to begin and persist with rehabilitation, particularly if you have to do it for yourself. Feelings can be your biggest obstacle. Some women find that feelings about the operation itself can get in the way. They would prefer to forget that it happened rather than accept it and take charge of their own healing.

Other feelings can include a sense of failure at not being able to achieve a vaginal birth, feelings about surgery in an area that still evokes embarrassment, worries about disfiguring scars, or just the general blues. When all of these combine, they raise a formidable barrier to any attempts to touch or even think about the operation site and scars. The truth is that what happened, happened. Your most important task right now is to help yourself heal.

Talking About It

If you find yourself having difficulty reading this chapter or in thinking about touching yourself, it will help to talk with other women. There are a growing number of groups of women in many regions of the country, books, and some individual counselors to help you. There is a resource guide at the end of this book.

Scar Mobilization

An incision long enough to accommodate your baby leaves a long scar. Even if the scar is low on your belly and scarcely visible, it could use some attention from you. Scar mobilization means just what it sounds like, moving the scar tissue around using simple massage techniques.

Why Do It?

Once your incision is healed, it's important to prevent the scar tissue from adhering to the muscle layers deeper inside. Remember that your incision penetrated all the way through skin, muscles, and uterus. Scar tissue can be quite deep.

When To Begin

You can begin to lightly massage your scar as soon as the incision has healed and the staples or stitches are out. Be gentle when you first begin, and if you feel any discomfort, stop and be much gentler. Your eventual goal is to move the skin and the muscles underneath so that they seem to slide freely over one another.

In most cases scar tissue with its tendency to adhere to muscle can be dealt with by you. Your scar can be lifted and separated from healthy muscle tissue to reduce or eliminate adhesion. This scar mobilization will actually reduce the amount of scar tissue. As you loosen the scar, it may also take away any feelings that you have of pinching or pulling in your lower belly as you reach for things on a high shelf .

There is no final time limit for working on scars. You can begin two years after a cesarean and still make the scar softer, thinner, and less visible.

How To Do It

Some people are reluctant to touch the scar or even the whole general area of the incision. If you feel this way, begin by lightly touching and stroking yourself, first with your palms and then with your finger tips. If this is too hard, begin by using a soft, clean cloth. Use a mirror to closely examine your scar. Nobody is going to be gentler or more thoughtful about your healing than you yourself.

Begin scar mobilization by rubbing your hands together to warm them up. You can use warm compresses or neutral oils, if they make you more comfortable or make the massage pleasanter, but they aren't necessary. If oil appeals to you, use a little, but don't make the skin so slippery that you can't get a good hold on the scar tissue.

Massage the scar tissue by working it with a rubbing motion along the grain (along the line of the scar).

Stroke back and forth against the grain (across the scar).

Roll the scar between your thumb and your forefinger.

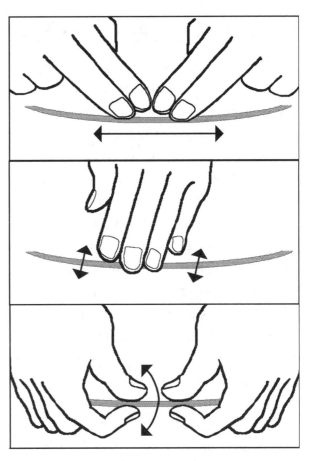

To get the maximum benefit, the massage should be done 2-3 times a day for 5-10 minutes at a time. The more you massage the scar, the more pliable, soft, thin, and cosmetically appealing it will become. Don't rub so hard that it hurts. At the end, hold the ends of the scar and gently push and pull it back and forth, and from side to side for a minute or two. You can expect to feel and see results in three to four weeks. Don't worry about not always doing the full time, every little bit will help.

Exercises For Abdominal Rehabilitation

All post-partum mothers, whether they have had a cesarean or a vaginal birth, experience stomach sag. Your uterus expands steadily over the months of pregnancy and spreads and stretches the muscles of the abdomen. After the birth, your uterus begins to return to its original size, but the surrounding abdominal muscles are still stretched out and slack. Mothers who have undergone the operation have the additional problem of incisions that may have severed some of these muscles.

Healthy stomach muscles are absolutely essential for a healthy back. Over the next several years you are going to do an enormous amount of lifting and carrying and you want you to be free of pain while you do it. You can start building the strong stomach muscles you'll need right now. As soon as you have healed from your incision you the chapter on the abdominal muscles on page 61 of this book and begin th abdominal exercises. They will help you restore muscle tone and regain belly strength.

Caution - Cesareans and Your Pelvic Floor

Even though your baby did not pass through the birth canal, it's possible that the muscles, ligaments, or nerves in the pelvic floor may have been injured. During pregnancy, the labor process, and, possibly during the operation itself, there may have been injuries that could leave you with pain or other problems.

You carried your baby for nine months straining the pelvic floor and postural muscles. You also had hormonal changes that have loosened ligaments. You also probably pushed for some time before the operation. These may have caused pelvic floor injuries which may have been overlooked because we incorrectly assume that cesareans don't cause pelvic injury. In addition, the surgery may have left scar adhesions that interfere with the nerves that supply the muscles of the pelvic floor.

If you experience any of these symptoms: pain in the pubic symphysis (where your pubic bones come together at the front); pain in or around the labia, along the inner thighs, or within your vagina; or, if you suspect a prolapse (feel an internal sagging within or above your vagina); or if you have urinary or fecal incontinence, these may be the result of a birth related injury and should be brought to the attention of your health care provider.

The next chapter in this book will give you some specific descriptions of possible birth injuries and some help with rehabilitation both by exercise and massage.

A Last Word

If you've had a cesarean, you are certainly not alone. And you certainly shouldn't feel guilty. You have done your best under difficult circumstances. The reasons for the frequency of this operation in the United States are complex and confusing. A VBAC (Vaginal Birth After Cesarean) is a possibility for some women. If you have questions about the cesarean procedure, or a VBAC for your next birth, talk it over with your health care provider and do some investigating on your own.

> **TIP: The cesarean surgical procedure and the particular anesthetics used can result in very unpleasant gas pain. Do this for relief:**
> - **Lie on your back with knees up and rock from side to side.**
> - **Lie on your left side as much as possible (reduces pressure on your sigmoid colon).**
> - **Use heat on the right side of the abdomen while you lie on the left.**
> - **Use a TENS unit (these are described on page 161).**

Strengthening the Pelvic Floor

Strong pelvic floor muscles are vital to a woman's health and sense of well being. You can imagine the pelvis as a wide topped funnel with the muscles of the pelvic floor making a sling across the bottom opening. Since these muscles support the bladder, the uterus, and the rectum they are essential for bowl and bladder functioning. They surround and support the vagina and so contribute to the enjoyment of sex.

The child bearing year takes its toll on these muscles. Hormonal changes, the baby's weight, and the loosening of the joints and ligaments during pregnancy cause stretching and stress. Labor and vaginal delivery can further stress and even tear them. Episiotomies done during delivery may leave nerve damage and scarring.

Cesareans can also disturb the muscles of the pelvic floor. "How can I have pelvic floor problems when the baby came out through an opening in my belly?" is a good question. Pelvic floor problems are not common after cesarean deliveries, but they do occur. An abdominal incision can irritate the nerves that serve the pelvic floor muscles. Irritated nerves may send signals that cause the muscles to chronically contract, and over-contracted, fatigued muscles will ache. This can make sexual intercourse painful (dyspareunia) in certain positions and may contribute to other pelvic floor problems.

Personal Issues

One obstacle that you may have to overcome, if this chapter is going to help you, is embarrassment. In spite of the changes in our attitudes toward our bodies over the last few decades, embarrassment and the feeling of taboo linger on. Being able to look at, touch, and think about your **UNMENTIONABLES!** is essential for your health and well-being. You may need to giggle or even shudder, but please push through and beyond any feelings you have about your genitals, anus, and crotch. Your recovery and your future health are much more important. A hand mirror and some private time are a good way to begin getting acquainted with yourself.

Incontinence In The Early Weeks

The birth process may cause a temporary loss or diminishing of sensation in your genitals. Don't be alarmed if this happens to you. Urinary or fecal incontinence is also common. Dribbling or wetting when you laugh, sneeze, cough, or move vigorously is known as stress incontinence. Frequent trips to the bathroom during the day and night are known as frequency or nocturnal incontinence. The inability to hold your urine after you know you need to go is called urge incontinence. These are common problems during the first week or two after the birth. If you already had problems with incontinence during adolescence, you have a greater likelihood of having them again during your post-partum period.

Continued Incontinence

If stress or frequency incontinence persist for more than two weeks, your pelvic floor muscles may have been overstretched or damaged. You should consult with your health care practitioner, and read this chapter carefully.

Sex - Are You Kidding?

For most women sexual intercourse is the farthest thing from their minds during the early post-partum period. This is normal. Later on, if you find yourself not enjoying sex because of a lack of sensation or discomfort, you should suspect a problem with the pelvic floor muscles or with the nerves that supply them. In almost all cases, the conditions can be improved with simple exercises.

You may experience pain when inserting a tampon, diaphragm, or during sexual intercourse. Such pain can be the result of a tightly stiched episiotomy, tear, or a separation at the symphasis pubis where the pubic bones come together. If there was nerve damage during the birth, there can be a reflexive spasm of the pelvic floor muscles that causes discomfort or pain in the genital area.

Pain may radiate down the legs. Sometimes tight muscles force the coccyx (your tailbone) too far forward causing low back pain or pain during intercourse. Like other pelvic floor problems, this can often be alleviated with exercise and physical therapy techniques.

> **TIP: Pain radiating down the legs can also be a symptom of sacroiliac, lumbar spine or disc problems. You should consult with your health care practitioner if you are experiencing this symptom.**

Everything Is Falling Out!

A small percentage of women experience more serious problems. The pelvic floor muscles can become so severely stressed that they no longer support your internal organs well. When this happens, one of three problems may occur: cystocele, rectocele, or uterine prolapse.

The symptoms are commonly described as, "my insides are falling out," "it feels like sitting on a golf ball," "pressure and pain in my pelvis," "my vagina aches deep inside," or "I have trouble with constipation or starting my urine stream." Since these sensations can also describe other medical conditions, you should consult with your health care practitioner if you experience them.

NORMAL

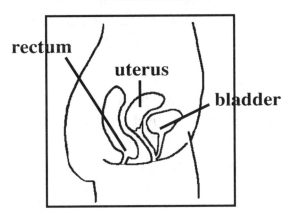

This diagram shows you how the bladder, uterus, and rectum normally lie within your pelvis.

CYSTOCELE

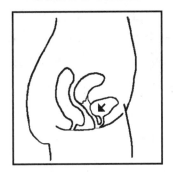

If the muscles and tissues supporting the bladder are stretched too far, the bladder will press down into the vagina. This is known as a cystocele.

RECTOCELE

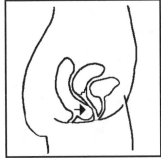

If the rectum bulges into the wall of the vagina from behind, it is called a rectocele.

UTERINE PROLAPSE

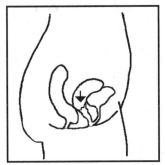

When the uterus is not held in place by the pelvic floor muscles and its own supporting ligaments, it can protrude into the vagina. This is called a uterine prolapse.

Pelvic floor problems range from the embarrassing and the slightly discomforting to the physically incapacitating. Almost all are easily treated and improved. Taking care of problems now will have immediate benefits and prevent greater problems later on. There are a variety of treatments available and they depend on the severity of your condition. With exercises and biofeedback training most women can strengthen their own pelvic floor muscles. You can decrease pain, weakness, and the "everything is falling out" feeling, and as well as correct incontinence.

Some of these conditions can sound pretty grim. Don't give up! Only the most severe cystoceles, rectoceles, or prolapses (and these are rare) require surgery. Most problems are the result of slack, overtaxed, or slightly damaged pelvic floor muscles or weakened ligaments and can be treated with simple physical therapy techniques. A careful evaluation by a physical therapist, midwife, gynecologist, or urologist will help you decide upon a course of rehabilitation.

Seek out a medical practitioner you trust and who is sympathetic to new mothers. Unfortunately, some professionals have been known to dismiss problems with "what did you expect from having a baby," or, "that goes with the turf." If you encounter this attitude, seek help elsewhere. You deserve competent and sympathetic medical attention. The chapter on seeking professional help (page 164) and the resources section (page 178) will help you with your search.

Getting In Touch With Your Pelvic Floor

Here's a simple way to make contact with the muscles of your pelvic floor:

The perineal body is the area that lies in between your vagina and your anus. Place your finger tips on there. Then cough. Do you feel the perineal body move down against your fingers?

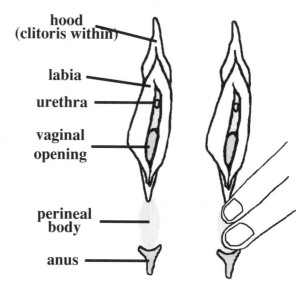

Most women will feel it pushing down. The push is from the downward force of the internal organs on the muscles of the pelvic floor. What you should feel is a lifting up. When the muscles pull up and in, they strengthen and protect the pelvic floor. This is what you are going to learn to do. Begin with the Kegel exercises.

The Kegel Exercises

Arnold Kegel, M.D. was an American obstetrician/gynecologist who worked extensively with incontinent women. He recognized that the pelvic floor muscles were strained during childbirth and that they needed strengthening and rehabilitation in the same way as any other part of the body that has suffered either trauma or overexertion. Kegel gave a great deal of thought to the treatment of these vital muscles and devised a series of exercises to help heal them. He also developed a simple biofeedback device for helping women visualize the exercise.

Getting Started (sometimes it's hard)

Although the Kegel exercises are simple, they have proved hard for many women to learn. Much of the problem is identifying and isolating the muscles so that you can begin to exercise them.

People mistakenly thought of the pelvic floor muscles as if they were locked away deep inside the body. These "hidden" muscles had to be imagined. Women were asked to think of their pelvic floor as an elevator and lift it up, or to imagine pulling the walls of the vagina together, or to visualize writing the alphabet with their pelvic floor. These images, whether silly or poetic, don't really help much because no amount of elevator lifting is going to work if you can't locate the buttons or don't know which floor you want. Once you learn about your pelvic floor muscles and how to locate them, they are easy to exercise.

More About Those Muscles

The muscles of the pelvic floor are a wonderful solution to a complicated problem. The problem is to provide a strong and flexible base for your internal organs. The base also supports the weight of your growing baby, allows the normal passage of body wastes, permits sexual function, and is able to expand enough to accommodate the passage of the newborn. In the picture on the right you can see a side view of the pelvic floor. This cup shaped sling is formed by webs and straps of strong, flexible muscle and ligament.

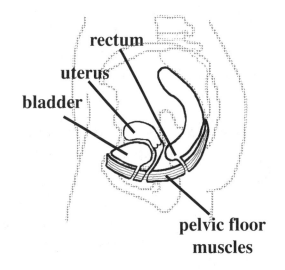

Cup your hands one on top of the other, palms up, in your lap. When you look down into it, you'll see a good model of your pelvic floor.

How To Locate The Muscles

Here are some ways to visualize the pelvic floor muscles. Each can be the start of the Kegel exercises. If none of them work for you, you will find other ways described later in this chapter.

- Imagine that you are at a crowded party and have a sudden urge to pass gas. Tighten up the muscles around your anus and vagina to hold it back. Hold these muscles tight for a count of three. Relax them. Repeat twenty-five times.

- Imagine that you have just sneezed and feel an urgent need to pass gas. Pull in around the muscles of the pelvic floor to prevent it and then let go and tighten again. Repeat these quick flickers of contraction twenty-five times.

- Try imagining the muscles you use to stop your flow of urine. These muscles lie around the anus, vagina, and urethra, so pulling up on them pulls in the skin around this area as well. Imagine holding the skin and tissues up and inside for a count of three. Relax, then repeat twenty-five times.

- Imagine that your partner's penis or finger has entered your vagina and you grab hold of it with your vaginal muscles to pull it further inside.

As you try using these images, place the tips of your fingers on your perineum. If you can feel the perineum lift up, then you have located the muscles and can control them enough to do the Kegel exercises on your own.

The Kegel Exercises Themselves

If you've found the pelvic floor muscles and can feel your perineum lift, you're already doing the Kegel exercises. Even if you don't have pelvic floor problems, do them anyway. Whether or not you plan to have more children, they will help you throughout your life. Make a time each day to do them, and also do them at odd moments, like while you're driving.

If you do have pelvic floor problems, you should work with a health care practitioner to establish an exercise program suited to your needs. The exercises are simple and can only be beneficial, so if there is no professional help available, just go ahead on your own until you can talk with someone. Three ten to twenty minute sessions a day would be a good beginning for a woman with moderate problems.

> **TIP: The Kegel exercises are the most important part of this chapter. For many women they will be the most important part of this book.**

Caution - Interrupting The Urine Flow

Women are sometimes counseled to interrupt the flow of their urine as a way of exercising the pelvic floor muscles. Urine interruption does use these muscles, but it's not the best way to get them into shape. Here are three reasons why:

- If your muscles are weak or damaged, you may be unable to interrupt the flow. Failure can be discouraging and you may give up trying.

- Interruption is an extremely inefficient method of exercising the muscles involved. It's been estimated that recovery from moderate stress incontinence would require you to interrupt the flow of your urine three hundred times a day for seven to nine weeks. That's a lot of time on the toilet!

- Some studies have suggested that excessive or prolonged interruption can cause urine to back up into the bladder. This can cause urinary tract infections.

Interrupting your urine flow is useful as a way of locating the pelvic floor muscles, just don't do it frequently. Use the mental image of interruption to practice contracting the muscles. You can also try stopping the flow once a month to see how you progress. If you can't interrupt the flow at all, don't give up! Get someone to help you.

Exercising the Pelvic Floor Muscles

The muscles that make up your pelvic floor contain two kinds of muscle fiber, slow twitch and fast twitch. As you can probably guess, slow twitch fibers give muscles strength and endurance, and fast twitch fibers deliver a quick response. Both kinds of fiber are important to pelvic floor health. Each kind of fiber requires a squeeze, but to exercise the whole muscle you need both kinds of squeezing.

Slow Holds (for slow fibers)

Research has shown that a series of strong, steady squeezes for 8 to 10 seconds, alternating with short periods of rest, works best. Try to do 40 - 80 squeezes over the day. Remember, a steady squeeze builds slow fiber strength.

Quick Flicks (for fast fibers)

Coughs, sneezes, and sudden bursts of laughter are where the fast twitch fibers take over. In between slow squeezes, do 2 quick squeeze and releases. You'll discover that you soon begin to anticipate the need to squeeze as part of the urge to sneeze. Before long, you'll do this automatically.

All Together Now!

Like any set of exercises, it's easiest to develop a routine that you can fall back on without thinking. A basic unit of 10 slow strengthening squeezes followed by two quick squeeze and release works best. It may seem like a chore at first, but you'll quickly get into it, and you'll get lifetime benefit.

When to Squeeze?

- **Squeeze before you sneeze.**

- **Squeeze and lift when you get up from sitting.**

- **Squeeze when you lift your baby.**

Pessaries

Pessaries are simple, doughnut like devices (they come in different sizes and shapes) used as an alternative to immediate surgery for a prolapsed uterus. Pessaries are inserted through the vagina where they rest behind the pubic bone. It fits over the cervix and supports the uterus in its correct position. Your health care practitioner will prescribe the correct size and shape and teach you how to put it in place.

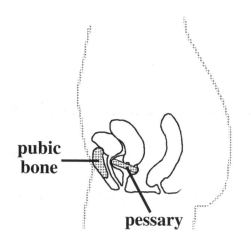

They are usually prescribed as an alternative to immediate surgery or until the child bearing years are over. If you have a prolapse that requires the use of a pessary, the Kegel exercises will not be enough to rehabilitate your pelvic floor muscles. They will still be beneficial, however, and you can do them with the pessary inserted.

Depending on the severity of prolapse, some women wear a pessary only during sports activity, others wear them when standing and active on their feet for long periods, and others wear them all day long.

> **TIP: Whenever you lift or strain to do something, remember to tighten your lower belly muscles (see the Abdominal chapter!) and squeeze at the same time. Imagine pulling in your belly as if you were zipping up tight pants while you squeeze and pull up your pelvic floor.**

Electrical Stimulation

Electrical stimulation is sometimes used in muscle rehabilitation when a muscle is weakened by nerve damage. Damaged nerves send few or no impulses at all to a muscle and an underused muscle weakens or atrophies. Your physician or a physical therapist may use electrical stimulation to keep the muscles in good shape while natural recovery occurs. The length and number of treatments varies.

Abdominal Exercises and The Basic Breath

After your pelvic floor muscles begin to recover, pay attention to your abdominal muscles. As long as you find yourself pushing out your lower belly and pelvic floor when you exert yourself, avoid anything too strenuous and sit ups in particular. You will be ready for more ambitious exercises after you learn the "basic breath" described here and the exercises in the chapter on the abdominals (p.61).

Why Learn The Basic Breath?

Almost all of us have acquired the bad habit of holding our breath and pushing down on the pelvic floor when we exert ourselves. The "basic breath" exercise will re-educate your muscles so that your pelvic floor and lower back are protected and strengthened each time you push, pull, or lift.

The Basic Breath

Start by lying down on your back, arms out to the sides, and bring your knees up by sliding your feet toward your bottom. Think about your belly muscles and then practice sucking them in and releasing them a few times. Relax a moment.

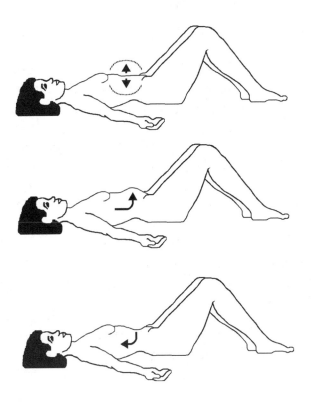

Then, breathe in. The belly fills and rises, everything expands.

As you breathe out, pull in everything below the belly button. Repeat the cycle several times. Don't tilt your pelvis or let your back flatten; keep the natural curve of your lower back.

The Basic Lift

Lift your baby and notice what happens. Do you hold your breath when you pick up your child, or push down on your pelvic floor, or puff your lower belly out? If you do, you need to re-educate your muscles. Practicing the "basic breath" every time you lift anything is a perfect way to begin.

Follow these steps each time you lift:

- **Breathe in**, stomach relaxes and expands.

- **Breathe out**, stomach pulling in.

- **Lift** (and keep breathing out as you do).

As you lift, or do anything that requires a sudden effort, pull your abdominal and pelvic floor muscles in and up while you let your breath out.

A Last Word – Don't Give Up!

There are several reasons why you may find it hard to gain control of the pelvic floor muscles.

- It's common to lose some sensation in the vaginal area after giving birth. You may not be able to tell whether you are contracting the muscles or not.

- Many of us have never consciously used the pelvic floor muscles to pull up and in. We don't know what it feels like.

- Many women have some pelvic floor weakness already. This means that it's difficult to identify and exercise the muscles, and it's tempting to give up in frustration.

- You may have an adhered (stuck down) episiotomy scar or other birth injury that makes the pelvic floor painful.

- Many people are still embarrassed about their bodies.

All of these are obstacles to your healing. Don't let any of them stop you. With time, proper care, and a strong and healthy concern for your own well-being, each can be overcome. You (and your pelvic floor) deserve to be in the best of health.

> **TIP: The best mother's day present that you can give yourself is to read this chapter thoroughly and learn how to do the Kegel exercises. If you have a daughter, teach her the Kegel exercises.**

The Changing Table

Raising children is hard work. Parenting involves physical labor and the risk of physical injury. For some of us, these physical injuries are minor aches and pains. For others, they may be more serious and more painful. For those with chronic physical problems, the risks are greater.

All of us can safely manage our day to day work as parents. It's possible to remain free of pain, or, if you are in pain, you can learn how to prevent further injury while your body heals.

Since you are going to have a long and busy relationship with diapers, changing tables are good places to start taking care of yourself. By the time your baby is two, you will have changed around four thousand diapers at all hours of night and day, whether you felt like it or not. That's a lot of bending, lifting, hunching over, picking up, bending over again, and putting down. It's good sense to have this be as safe and as comfortable as possible.

Making Your Job Safer and Easier

When you stop and think about any activity there are two elements to consider. One is how you do it and the other is what you do it with. This is as true for the use of the changing table as it is for flying an airplane.

How You Do It

The hurried movement of snatch and lower used to take a child from the changing table is a good example of how an ordinary task can cause pain. When you twist and lift or twist and lower at the same time, you force your spine (and the muscles that support it) to fight one another; the loser is you. Twisting and lifting at the same time is the worst possible combination of movements for your spine. It makes you vulnerable to everything from badly pulled muscles to herniated vertebral discs.

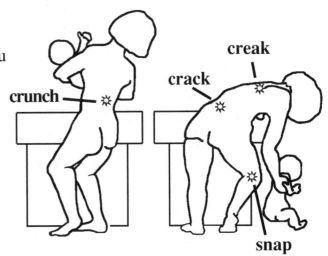

> **TIP: Lift, take a breath, then move your feet to begin your turn.**

All of us snatch and lower unthinkingly and it's the kind of bad motion habit that eventually catches up with us. You can change this. Learn to think of things as a series of steps. When you think of an action in slow motion, any steps that may be harmful to you will become obvious. You can alter them or you can break them down into even smaller, more manageable steps.

Look closely at the sequence of pictures below. They show how to lift and lower without strain without twisting and lifting all at once. Lift step by step, use your legs to turn, and then lower your child.

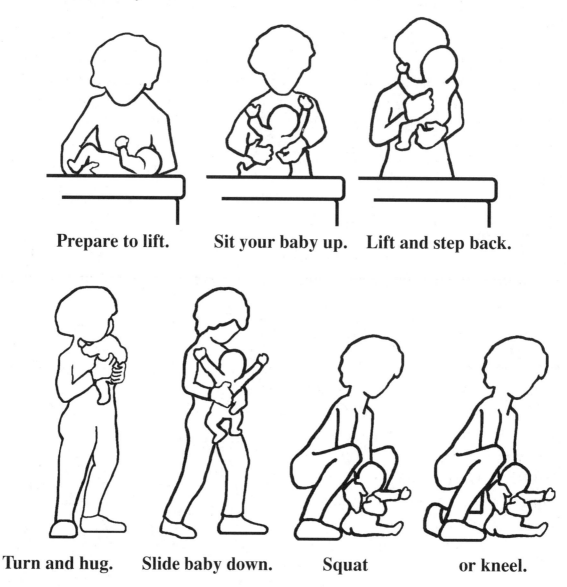

Prepare to lift.   **Sit your baby up.**   **Lift and step back.**

Turn and hug.   **Slide baby down.**   **Squat**   **or kneel.**

It doesn't take any longer to do this and it will save you from hours of pain.

TIP: When you lift, lower, or squat tighten your lower belly muscles. The chapter on the abdominal muscles (page 61) explains how and why.

What You Do It With

Most of the common things that we use come in standard sizes. These sizes have been established for "average" people. Since most of us aren't exactly average, we make do with things that aren't exactly right for us. Usually we manage to get by, but with the extra stress and hard work of parenting, or when your back already aches, small differences can add up to big pains.

The changing table is a good example.

| **Too high is hard on the upper back.** | **Too low strains the mid and lower back.** | **Waist height is just right for most people.** |

Modify your changing table to suit your needs. It might mean shortening the legs, putting it on something to make it higher, or getting a portable changing surface and setting it on something that makes it just right. Four thousand diapers (give or take) from now, you'll thank yourself.

Some people prefer to use their beds as a changing surface. Beds are comfortable, convenient, and don't take up any more room. The drawback to using a bed is its height. Standing next to a bed and changing a diaper bends you in just the wrong places.

If you use a bed, climb up on it yourself and kneel by your baby. If kneeling on both legs is a strain, kick off your shoes and bring one leg up. It'll take a bit longer, but it will protect your back. If your bed is low enough, kneel beside it.

Other Things You Can Do

If you have sacroiliac problems, keep a small block or box near your changing table. Rest one foot on it while you change your baby.

If you have any back problems at all, the hardest part is lifting a toddler back down from the table. Those last twelve inches down to the floor are the most dangerous. Keep something near that you can place your baby on. This gives you a moment to rest, reposition yourself, and will protect your back from further injury.

It could be a footstool, a step stool, or a short step ladder. When your child learns to climb, it will be a treat for your toddler, and a relief for you.

The two important lessons in this chapter are think about how you move and think about the equipment you use. The chapters Child Equipment, Step by Step, and Ergonomics take a closer look at some other day to day objects and tasks and how they can be made easier, better, and safer for you.

Child Equipment

Parents lead busy lives. In order to juggle the daily routine, the job, the house, and everything else, we need equipment that will occupy and protect our children without completely changing our homes around. We have child gates, walkers, and carriers of all kinds to get us through with a minimum of frazzle and a maximum of safety. These pieces of equipment are indispensable, but they can be tough on a parent's body.

Most of the equipment discussed in this chapter require lifting your child in and out. Lifting will be less hazardous when you learn some basic techniques. If you haven't already learned the "basic breath," turn to page 21 and learn it now, it'll only take a few minutes. Remember that it's neither bad nor dangerous for most people to lift. Most of our problems come from doing it over and over again or from lifting when we're too tired or distracted to do it carefully.

Child Gates

The child gate allows you to isolate areas in your house, block off stairs or dangerous spaces, and gives you (as much as anything can) peace of mind. The only danger from the child gate is to parents. There is a terrible temptation to save a few seconds and step over it. **Don't!** The awkward leg lift can stress or push your sacroiliac joint out of place. If this happens, the few seconds saved will be turned into hours of discomfort.

A Safer Way

Always open your childgate, never step over it, especially when you have something heavy. If you are carrying something, put it down. New mothers, women during their periods, and anyone with previous problems with their sacroiliac joint must be careful. The chapter on the sacroiliac joint on page 73 will explain why.

The main point is to always think about doing any task in the easiest (and safest) way possible for yourself. It may take a bit longer, but it will be worth every minute.

> **TIP: Read the chapter Step By Step next (on page 34) . It will help you find safe and easy ways to accomplish day to day tasks without injury.**

Swings

For some people these swinger/rockers make the difference between sanity and insanity during dinner preparation at the end of a busy day.

The two drawbacks are the shin or knee height level of the seat and the top of the frame. They keep you from getting close while you lift or lower your child into the seat. Stooping or bending over to put your baby in or take your baby out can put a tremendous strain on your back and knees.

A Safer Way

Kneel on one or both knees to get your baby in and out. It may seem harder to get down on the floor like this, but it's really much easier on your body. You can also try putting your baby into the swing by sliding her or him in from behind. Standing closer allows you to squat as you lower (or lift) rather than stoop.

Walkers

These are often the next step up from swings when your baby becomes a crawler, cruiser, or toddler. Not everyone recommends them because of possible accidents, particularly on stairs. They are also not completely secure as soon as your child is capable of climbing out of them. However, many people find them useful as long as they are nearby to keep an eye on things.

Walkers are hard to get children into and out of because you have to lift over the wide rim that surrounds the child. It's the same problem as swings only worse; you are tempted to stoop over and lean forward when you are picking them up. This is hard on the middle and lower back.

A Safer Way

You can straddle the walker and squat slightly to reach down for your child. This sounds awkward, but it is much safer than leaning over and lifting. Always bring your child in close to your body when you lift.

Cribs

The old fashioned, high standing cribs with drop sides are easy on the back. They stand high enough so that the baby is at about waist height and you can slide the baby in and out without bending and stooping over. On the other hand, you can't snap one of those monsters apart, fold it up, and stuff it in a sack to take with you for a weekend trip or an evening with friends. The portable crib is the answer for our more mobile life-style, but once again, the baby is too close to the ground for parent comfort.

A Safer Way

Bring the baby close to your body. To do this, gently roll or slide your baby to the side of the crib closest to you.

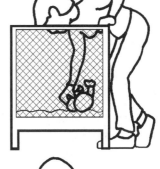

Then, bring your feet as far under the side as possible and push your knees close in. Since these cribs have fabric sides you can push in quite far. It helps to imagine your weight being carried on the bottoms of your feet with your buttocks stuck out for balance.

People with back problems often experience difficulty about half way between bending over and standing up straight. You can ease yourself through this place by letting your forearms rest on the edge of the crib. Take a moment to breathe, then roll the baby closer into your body along your arms to finish the lift.

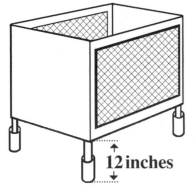

12 inches

There is another solution to the safe use of portable cribs. You can buy or construct yourself supports that fit under the legs of the crib and build it up. Studies have shown that if something is at least twelve inches above the ground, it's much easier on your back.

Strollers

The old fashioned baby carriage, the picture book kind, rolled the baby along at a perfect height for lifting in and out without much strain. But can you imagine getting that huge carriage onto a bus, up a mall escalator, or into the back of your car? So we have the easily pushed, collapsible, convenient, but too low strollers. Strollers share the stoop over problems of walkers and swings. It always seems quicker and easier to hunch over and to pick up — until something twinges in your lower back.

A Safer Way

The better way is to squat or kneel in front of the stroller and then slide your baby in. You can kneel on one or both legs depending on which is more comfortable. Most strollers have a place to carry things and you can stash something like a piece of foam or an old hand towel to protect your knees from the ground.

Taking the baby out is just the reverse. Squat or kneel, slide your baby into your arms, and then stand.

Buy the simplest, sturdy stroller that you can find. Some strollers have gotten so complicated that they are as awkward as the old baby carriages, but without the advantage of being high off the ground.

You can use the front and back wheels of the stroller to lever yourself up short flights of stairs. Tilt the stroller back and push it up to the first step. Lower the front wheels onto a higher step and lift the back. Roll the front wheels as far forward as you can and set the back wheels down one step higher. When you have steps that this will work with, it'll help you avoid the temptation to pick up the stroller and baby together (a real back strainer).

> **TIP: Protect your back when you lift your baby. Tighten your lower abdominal muscles (the ones below the navel) as you exhale and lift.**

Carriers and Backpacks

Backpacks, slings, and other carriers are necessary evils from the standpoint of back strain and pain. In spite of all claims, when you have extra weight stuck out in front, in back, or to the sides, the result is extra work for the muscles that hold you up. It can be work that won't cause you pain, if you follow a few simple guidelines.

A Safer Way

Start using the device early in your child's life. Use it frequently, but for short intervals when you start. This will allow you to work up to the time when your baby is bigger, more active, and you may want to carry her or him for longer periods.

Use good body mechanics and be careful when putting the pack on and taking it off. Get someone to hold it for you whenever possible. If you're getting it on by yourself, always place it on as high a surface as possible. Use a table or the hood of your car. (If your carrier has a metal frame, wrap the exposed metal at the bottom with either cloth tape or duct tape, to prevent scratching your furniture or your car hood.

Use your pack's waist strap. This distributes some of the weight onto your hips and makes it easier on your back. Shrug your shoulders a couple of times and do a gentle backwards stretch or two before and after using a back carrier. This stretch counteracts the pulling forward that your shoulders do when you wear a back carrier. It also stretches out the muscles across the front of the chest.

TIP: The simple standing backbend will do you a lot of good now and a lot more good later in life. Read about it and how to do it on page 90.

Slings

Soft carriers generally allow you to keep your child's weight closer to you and lower on your body. They also have the advantage of allowing you to shift the weight from front to back or side to side. Their disadvantage is that wearing them for long periods will distort your posture as you compensate for the extra weight.

A Safer Way

If you use a soft sling or side carrier, make sure that you do alternate sides each time you use it. Don't wear a front pack or front sling so low that your upper back is curved forward or so high that you are unbalanced. Alternating is always the key. After you've carried your baby in front for a while, switch to the back.

Fixed Car Seats

Children's car seats are an absolute necessity. They are required by law. Even if they weren't, you'd want to have one to protect your child. Their drawback is the extra work and potential strain of getting your child in and out of the car.

A Safer Way

There are two ways to handle the car seat problem. The first is to place the car seat in the center of the back seat. This makes it possible for you to sit next to your child while you lift him or her onto your lap. You can then slide over to the door, get both your feet out of the car and onto the street. Then stand up with the child held close.

The second is to place the seat next to the door so that you can reach right down into the seat and scoop your child up. Be sure you slide your child to the front edge of the seat before lifting.

If you have a van or larger car, it may be easier to kneel next to the child's car seat, bring the child in close to your body, and back out. A swiveling car seat has been developed and you might want to look into this.

Which seat position you use depends on your own physical needs. People with lower lumbar back strains might prefer the center location; people with sacroiliac problems might prefer the side location. You should probably experiment with both and find the one that's safest and most comfortable for you.

Whichever you use, remember to take your time. Pausing to take a breath before you move will give you a moment to think about lifting and where to place your feet.

Portable Car Seats

This sounds ridiculous to say, but the main problem with portable car seats is that you have to carry them. Because of their shape, the weight (seat plus child) has to be held far out to the side, a great distance from your own center of gravity That puts stress on bones and muscles. If you crook your elbow through the carrier bar to bring it closer, you also cock your wrist at a dangerous angle (and you're probably carrying something else in that hand as well).

They are convenient, but they are tough on backs, shoulders, and wrists.

A Safer Way

The best solution is to carry your child next to your body with one arm while carrying the car seat with the other arm. Or, you can cradle the child in the seat in front of you with both arms. Even this isn't perfect for your body, though, and you can't carry anything else. If you have to carry the seat with the child in it with one arm, try to alternate sides frequently.

TIP: There are always new things on the market that promise to make your life easier and your child safer. Sometimes they do both. Safety seats and car safety belts are two that do. Please, remember to buckle both of you up. Everything else, try before you buy.

Step By Step

Rush, rush, rush. It's the lucky parent who only has six things to do at once. As a parent you quickly learn to talk on the phone while spreading peanut butter, offering a knee to a sobbing toddler with a runny nose, keeping an eye on the stove, and wondering if the load in the washer is done, all at the same time.

Most of our frazzling multiple activities can be accomplished - with a little practice. But some activities, particularly those that involve moving different parts of your anatomy in different directions all at the same time, are difficult and potentially dangerous. Lifting and turning all at once is one example. Breaking activities into simple steps that you do one at a time almost always makes them easier and safer. You can use this step by step method for everything you do.

A Dangerous Leap

Just getting up in the morning is a good place to begin. When we get up from bed or off the floor a lot of us have a tendency to snap straight up.

When you look at this action in slow motion, it's clear why it's dangerous.

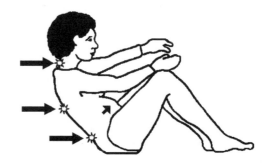

When you come straight up the abdominal muscles are pushed out into a stretched and weakened position. This puts a major strain on the lower back. Even with the support of your arms, the upper back curves forward dangerously, the neck is strained, and the lower back is at risk.

A good test for any activity like this is to ask yourself, can I do it slowly? If you can't, it means you shouldn't do it without some preparation. If you have recently given birth, are having your period, or have any back problems, don't do it at all.

Thinking In Steps

When you imagine doing something slowly, you automatically break it down into steps. Then you can look at each step and see if it works for you. If it doesn't, you can figure out a different way of doing whatever it is.

This is a better solution to the getting up problem:

Bring your knees up. **Roll over onto your side.** **Push up with your arms.**

Squat and rise. **Or kneel and rise.**

You can come up on both legs or one, whichever is more comfortable. Exhale and tighten the lower abdominal muscles as you stand.

This works just as well when you are getting up from bed. Swing your feet onto the floor after you push up with your arms. If you have or have had back problems, be careful about how you stand up from a sitting position. Bring your feet under you as far as possible and turn slightly to the left or right as you rise up.

Leaping into things (or out of things, or onto things) isn't the best idea for new mothers. Your body is recovering from lots of hard work and your hormones are still in flux. Both of these make you more vulnerable to muscular injuries.

> **TIP: The muscles of the lower belly and pelvic floor play a crucial role in keeping your lower back safe. Learn to breathe out and tighten them as you exert yourself in any situation. The chapter on the abdominal muscles on page 61 will teach you how.**

Lifting Step by Step

Lifting is something parents do more than almost anybody. So it's a good place to start applying the step by step method.

Getting groceries into and out of the back of the car is a great example. It's something we all do frequently—and, all too often, we run the risk of muscle strain.

A Better Way

• Get your feet as far under the load as possible.

• Bend your knees, exhale, and bring the load up to a more manageable height.

• Rest your load on the edge of the car.

• Reposition yourself so that you can lift the weight as close to your body as you can. Remember to keep the natural curve in your lower back.

• Exhale each time you lift and tighten the muscles in your lower abdomen.

OK, so we cheated a little. If your child's tantrum gets in the way of being sensible about lifting that bag, deal with your child first. Then get the groceries.

Breaking actions down into steps may seem to take longer. Sometimes it does—maybe ten seconds more. Not long at all compared with an hour's wait in the doctor's office and a couple of days of bed rest!

TIP: No matter how you lift, it is an effort. Use different ways of lifting during the day. It spreads the work to other parts of your body. It's easier to heal from a lot of small aches than from a major disaster.

Ergonomics

Ergo-WHAT?

Ergonomics is the science of making things fit people. It's a fancy word for a very common sense idea.

Imagine a seven-year old trying to drive a car. Her legs aren't long enough to work the pedals and she's not tall enough to see over the dashboard. This is because cars aren't ergonomically designed for seven-year old people.

The Myth Of The Perfectly Average Person

As you look around at the world with ergonomic eyes you'll begin to notice a lot of things that were not built with you in mind. Mass produced items like stoves and chair seats are made to fit the so called average person. Average means taking everything from the most to the least and figuring out what's in the middle. Naturally, only a few of us fall right in the middle and are "average." The rest of us are too short or too tall, too thin or too plump, too much of something to allow a completely comfortable fit.

The Perfectly Average Pain

If you're very un-average as a person, the chances are that you've already made some changes in your environment. Left-handed people buy special tools, and basketball players don't buy little cars.

Most of us, however, fall close enough to the average to keep us from thinking about modifying things. We assume that we are the mystical, all-American average person. So we stoop a little too much here, strain to reach a little bit too much there, and generally force our bodies to fit into situations that were designed for somebody just a little bit taller or shorter than us. Because of all the stooping, straining, and slouching we wind up either uncomfortable or in real pain.

> **TIP: Think of yourself as unique and special, not average.**
> **Then shape your environment to your unique and special needs.**

Comfort First!

Every new parent has endless demands to meet. There is always stress of one sort or another and lots of sleepless nights. Any and all comforts are important, no matter how small. A chair that's only an inch or two high, a pillow that's just a little too thin, or a computer monitor that's tilted too low, can make the difference between comfort and discomfort. It's a good time to be selfish. You deserve to feel well.

It's Not Just Furniture

Using ergonomics means making your whole environment fit you. It's not just the height of a chair seat, but light, temperature, and space as well. It involves all aspects of your being comfortable and healthy in your home or workplace. It also involves any and every other place where you spend time.

The quality of your lighting is a great example. Whether you're working with a dim computer display or squinting to read the instructions for assembling a portable crib under a dim bulb, you'll find yourself unconsciously bending forward and tipping your neck at an awkward angle so that you can see better. Poor lighting can be as bad for your neck and upper back as it is for your eyes.

Making Yourself Comfortable

Think of your day as three equal parts, one for sleeping, one for working, and one for home. Each of these parts of the day has its own stresses. It's up to you to put the comfort back in. Ask a few questions about how comfortable things really are for you. Then think about how to shape your environment to fit.

At Night

You spend about a third of each day in bed. Since your body may take several months to completely recover from pregnancy and birth, it's an important third. Is your bed comfortable? Too hard? Too soft? Too wide? Too narrow? Are your pillows right for you? Are there lumps in your mattress? Are you too hot or cold at night? Do you wake up with more aches and pains than when you went to bed? Do you always sleep on the same side? These may seem like trivial questions, but they aren't. Your sleep is important. You can make changes that will make it better.

At Work

The next third of your day is spent at work. Whether you're at home or at a job, you're working. And two questions you should keep asking yourself about everything, "how comfortable am I," and "how safe am I?"

When we look back in history, we see the nightmare working conditions of our industrial past. The old cotton mills filled with choking dust and the unprotected steel mills with their deafening sounds and searing heat are disappearing. However, they have been replaced with newer workplace hazards. If you are a working parent, the environment in which you spend most of your day is crucial to your well being.

Is your workplace safe? Is your office furniture suited to your particular physical needs? Is your desk the right height? Do the pedals of the machine you operate come within easy reach? Is your display screen too high, too low, too bright? Do you sit the same way hour after hour? Is there one thing that you do over and over again? Are the chemicals you use safe?

At Home

If you have an outside job, a third of your day is spent in your home. If you are at home during the day, then the home environment is even more important. Julia Child, the zestful television chef, is over six feet tall and her TV kitchen was built for her height and reach. Most cooks don't have a scenic department ready to build their kitchens and have to make do with standard size "average" equipment. It's this equipment that it's important to ask questions about.

Taller cooks stoop over average stoves and sinks and counters.

Shorter cooks have to hunch up their shoulders to reach into pots and strain on tip-toes to reach high shelves and refrigerator tops.

Any cook will benefit from changes that make the work more comfortable.

Is your changing table the right height? Do you always have to squat to get the baking dish you want? Do you get a pain between the shoulder blades after washing the dinner dishes? Do you hunch over counter tops? Do you keep frequently used foods or drinks in the bottom part of your refrigerator so that you have to stoop each time to get them? All of these can be changed with your comfort as your goal.

Different Strokes For Different Folks

Parents are often of different sizes. The differences may be nice, but the furniture can be a problem. Counter tops that are just right for the tall person are uncomfortably high for the short. Chairs which are low and comfortable for the short parent will be awkward for the tall one.

The differences may be occasionally discomforting or annoying, but not big enough to do anything about - most of the time. However, during pregnancy and throughout the post-partum period your body will be under unusual stress and the differences can be painfully magnified. The solution is to figure out who does what most of the time. Working surfaces and furniture should be adjusted to meet that person's physical needs.

Remember, changing little things can add up to big differences. With each small change you reduce stress and give yourself a feeling of accomplishment.

Three Things You Can Do To Help Yourself

- **Put yourself first.** Putting yourself first may seem like an obvious thing to do, but it can require an extra bit of speaking out on your part. Don't suffer silently even about little things.

- **Put yourself second**. If you need a chair that's higher or lower, don't hesitate to get one. It makes sense to have "your" chair. It always makes sense to shape your living environment to meet your needs.

- **Make each task safe for yourself**. Some chores should be given over to your partner during times when you are feeling physically vulnerable. For example, removing a heavy wet wash from a low front loader could be done more safely by somebody else when your pelvis is unstable.

A Simple Idea

Most of the things you use can (and should) be modified or rearranged to suit your individual ergonomic needs. A whole book could be written with specific suggestions about how to do this, but most are based on one simple idea. It is this, you are the best person to figure out how to make yourself comfortable.

Carrying

Doing It Safely

Football Carry

    This works great with newborns, but later on it's hard on wrists. Protect your wrists by alternating sides frequently. You can also grasp a cloth or some part of your child's clothing in the fingers of your supporting hand (this keeps you from bending the wrist too far in). You'll find more specific information on strengthening and caring for your wrists in the chapter on wrists on page 129.

Hip Carry

    This is a good carry when you want to use one hand to do something. It doesn't work for travelling any great distance. Be careful not to exaggerate the amount that your hips cock out to support your child's weight, and remember to shift from hip to hip so that both sides do equal work.

Front Carry

    The front carry protects your wrists, but you can't do anything else! It's comfortable and the body to body closeness makes it very satisfying. As you walk along, however, remind yourself not to get into a toe-out waddle. This will tire your lower back. You should also be careful to pull back your shoulder blades once in a while so you don't get into a round shouldered stoop.

Shoulder Carry

    Another good carry for comforting closeness. It's harder when your baby gets bigger simply because the extra weight shifts your center of gravity more and puts more of a strain on your back. Balance the work load by using each shoulder equally. If your baby tends to lean away from you, try the technique described on the next page.

Huggers And Sprawlers

Some children like to hug and be held close as they're carried, others like to sprawl over backwards, hang loose, and check out the world. Huggers are easy to carry. Sprawlers can be a chore. When the weight you are carrying leans away from your body, it's always extra work.

You can get a sprawler to hug some of the time with this technique.

Bring their upper body close to yours with a light hug or nuzzle and place their hands on your shoulders.

Grasp your child at the knees and begin to lift. As the child leans forward gently push the knees out slightly. The tilt into your shoulders will increase. Place one forearm behind their knees and keep them slightly bent by applying a gentle upwards pressure. It doesn't always work, but when it does, it will give your mid-back a chance to relax.

Temper Tantrums

Public temper tantrums are always difficult. You feel embarrassed, other people feel annoyed, and you'd probably like to just grab your child and get out of there. However, picking up a kicking and screaming little person is risky. Because of all the emotions (yours in particular) your body is tense. Meanwhile, the weight of your thrashing, angry child is going in all directions. Emotional tension and lifting awkward weights are a terrible combination. So, pause for a moment.

Then, instead of stooping and grabbing, get down to your child's level (physically, that is). Kneel or squat close and, if possible, hold your child close. Don't do any lifting yet. It may seem like an eternity when you get down to either soothe or give a child attention at his or her own level. But it won't be. Often taking the moment to stop and pay real attention to your child's distress (justified or not) will be calming. If it isn't and you have to make a fast exit, you'll already be in a better position to lift, and you won't be tempted to stoop and grab.

> **TIP: This is a time when counting to ten will save you lots of trouble.**

Sitting

Yes, Mom!

We are a nation of sitters. We sit to eat, watch television, talk with friends, feed our babies, and drive; and many of us sit for long hours at work. There's nothing wrong with sitting, the trouble comes from too much of it.

It is important (and possible) to rest your back while sitting. And it turns out (just like your mother told you) that sitting up straight is the best way to do it.

If your spine is too rounded or too flattened, then the muscles work harder and, by the end of the day, they'll begin to ache. When you lose the natural curve of the spine, one set of muscles becomes too slack and its matching set gets tight. Curving and straightening are natural. They happen with everything you do, with every move you make. The bad part comes when you do one or the other for too long and the muscles get stuck. This is as true for sitting as it is for everything else.

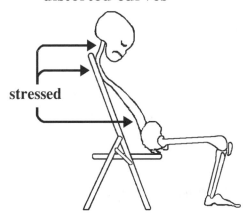

distorted curves

stressed

This exhausted looking person is making her body work even harder by slouching.

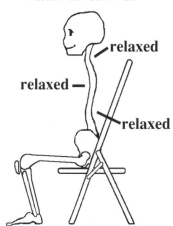

natural curves

relaxed

relaxed —

relaxed

This alert looking person is really getting more rest.

Learning to sit well is doubly important for working parents, since so many occupations now require you to be seated for long periods. The tensions of the workplace, the inability to move around freely, and the general fatigue felt by new parents all contribute to the kinds of muscle tension that will add up to a sore back unless you take good care of yourself.

> **TIP: Slump and then reach behind yourself to feel for your lumbar curve. You'll discover that it has almost completely disappeared.**

What You Sit On

Considering how much time we spend sitting, we spend very little time thinking about what we sit on. What you sit on determines how comfortably you sit. The right seat makes the difference between shoulder, hip, and back ache and no ache at all.

In the world of average chairs for average people, the chances are that you're not going to wind up with the completely perfect chair at home or at work (or at the PTA, movie theater, or wedding). So you need to take charge of your own sitting comfort.

Here are some things you can do:

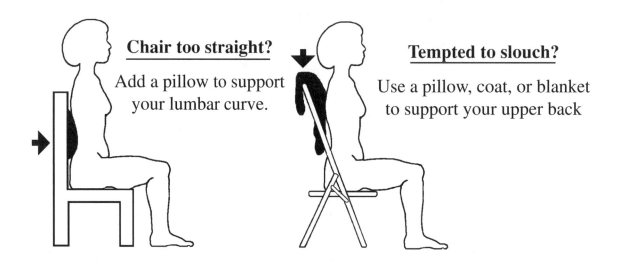

Chair too straight?

Add a pillow to support your lumbar curve.

Tempted to slouch?

Use a pillow, coat, or blanket to support your upper back

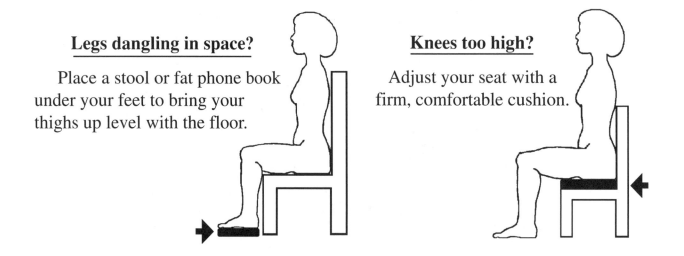

Legs dangling in space?

Place a stool or fat phone book under your feet to bring your thighs up level with the floor.

Knees too high?

Adjust your seat with a firm, comfortable cushion.

> **TIP: Always make your chair fit you.**

Perfectly Awful Chairs

After childbirth your abdominal muscles are overstretched and weakened. This means that your lower back is particularly vulnerable because the abdominal muscles do a lot to support your back. At the same time, your hormones are still adjusting. During late pregnancy, the hormonal balance favors those that loosen ligaments and make birth possible. Until your hormones return to normal, your joints will be unpredictably loose. Slight misalignments at places like the sacroiliac joints are more likely.

There are many chairs that will leave you wishing you'd never sat down. Some of the them are bad because the lack of support forces you to slump. This strains your lower back. Some of them are bad because they force your knees up higher than your pelvis. That strains your sacroiliac joint.

You'll save yourself a lot of discomfort if you avoid any chairs (or couches) that are soft, squishy, and low down enough to make it hard for you to get up. Use butterfly chairs, beanbag chairs, and soft, deep couches as little as possible.

The Perfect Chair

The perfect chair would support you comfortably in a sitting position that would not cause stress for any part of your body. It might look like the one shown here.

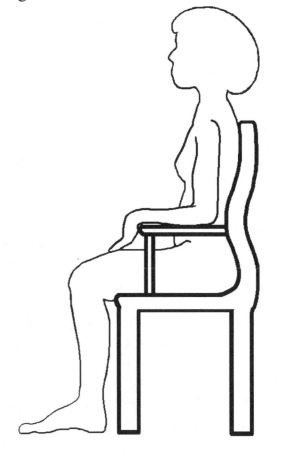

The seat cushion would be firm, but comfortable. Notice that the back of the knees are not pressed up against the edge of the chair. (If the front of your chair presses at the backs of your knees, use a pillow to push your whole body forward so that there is an inch or two of space.)

Most important of all is the back of the chair. It would follow the curve of the spine perfectly. This would give you perfect support (something you deserve everywhere in your life).

If there are armrests, they should be just slightly higher than the bottoms of your bent elbows. This will give you good support and keep your shoulders from drooping.

Getting Out Of The Chair

After you've been sitting for a long time getting up can be a problem. Coming straight forward, up, and out of a chair puts a considerable strain on back muscles. New mothers with overstretched, post labor, or post Cesarean belly muscles don't have the abdominal support necessary to make getting up easy and risk free.

Here are two ways to get out of a chair that will protect your back.

The first is to use a small, simple turn to the right or left when you get up. Slide to the front edge of the chair and place your hands on your thighs just above the knees. Turn slightly to one side or the other as you rise.

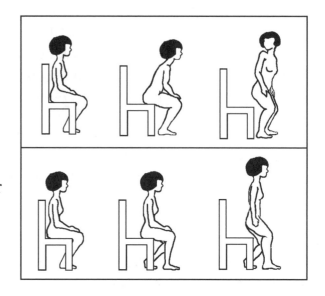

For the second, sit at the front of your chair. Slide one foot back so that it's under you and place the other foot a little forward. Stand straight up with the back leg doing the work. You can stand while keeping the natural curve of the spine.

In both cases, tighten the muscles of the lower belly before you begin to move.

Once You're Up

Many people experience stiffness or a crooked feeling in the lower back or pelvic area when they stand up after a long period of sitting.

To relieve this, stand about three feet from a wall and lean into it so that you're resting on your hands. Rock or tilt your pelvis back and forth.

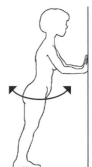

This pumps your spine and brings circulation both to the spine itself and the muscles and ligaments of the lower back and abdomen.

Since driving causes the same kind of muscle tightness, use this little exercise just after you get out of the car and before you lift your child out.

> **TIP: The chapter on the sacroiliac joint (page 73) has suggestions that will make sitting, seated work, and driving safer and more comfortable.**

Standing

Standing...You Mean Posture?

Groan... Does the very word posture bring up memories of parents and teachers pushing you up against walls, comparing you to rulers, and nagging at you to sit, lie, or stand up straight? "Posture" has so many bad associations that it might be better to forget the word altogether when talking about healthy and comfortable positions for your body. You should also forget all of the judgments,"slumped," "slouched," "good," and "bad," that may have been placed on you. Good posture should mean the ways in which your body can be as comfortable, flexible, and as vigorous as you want.

What Is Good Posture?

Good posture is dynamic. Your body is capable of lovely, flowing, relaxed, and easy movement. This has nothing to do with standing on a parade ground. In fact, this may be the problem with our idea of "posture." When we hear the word we imagine ourselves standing rigidly still, but in real life the human body is never still. Even when we try to be motionless, we expand and contract with each breath; veins and organs pulse and change, eyes move, and limbs shift. (Besides, as a parent, how often are you ever motionless?)

So, Why Do We Get So Bent Out Of Shape?

The strange, awkward, and uncomfortable postures that we get ourselves into and our poor habits of movement are not part of our original equipment. And they didn't just appear. They developed as part of our individual responses to the world. Many of them come from our reactions to emotional and physical stress.

The Feelings Part Of Posture

Our emotions often affect how we present ourselves physically. Imagine what you look like when you're feeling really depressed and "in a slump." Or take a look at yourself being angry in a full length mirror. Imagine stomping around all day holding that posture. You can see why the expressions "a pain in the neck," "a pain in the butt," and "sorehead" are often literally true.

TIP: Sometimes just taking a deep breath and allowing yourself a smile as you exhale will return your body to a comfortable posture.

The Physical Part Of Posture

Pain from a muscular injury can seriously affect your posture. When a person hunches over against pain and leans or bends to avoid stressing the sore area, it causes tightness and, sometimes, pain in other parts of the body. If the pain persists for a long time, these tense areas can become sites of chronic problems themselves.

Another physical cause of unhealthy posture is a subtle left/right size imbalance. One of our sides is usually a little bit bigger than the other. It's estimated that 60% of us are larger enough on one side to make a noticeable difference. Tilting or leaning slightly to compensate for a shorter leg length on one side puts a strain on muscles and joints. Wearing a smaller size shoe because it fits one foot and the other is 'just a little tight' creates foot and postural problems that can be very aggravating.

The Cultural Part of Posture

The world in which we live often molds us into unreasonable shapes. Adolescent girls often slump to avoid drawing attention to their breasts. The slumping may become habitual and continue in later life without any awareness that it causes back pain.

At the other extreme, our culture's idea of what is fashionable may push women into poses and outfits that can cause problems. High heels shorten the muscles at the back of the thigh and calf. Ordinarily, about half of the support you get for bending comes from the backs of the legs. With these muscles shortened most of the burden falls on the lower back which then must work twice as hard and can wind up hurting twice as much.

The Habit Part Of Posture

We are creatures of habit. We all get into ruts and do the same things in the same way over and over. Because of this we overwork some muscles and underwork others. You could call this "habitual stress." Although it can take a long time to accumulate, habitual stress can cause as much pain as a sudden injury. The cure is to become aware of our activities and vary them.

The Results Of Bad Posture

Here are two examples of bad posture. If either becomes chronic, there can be unpleasant physical consequences.

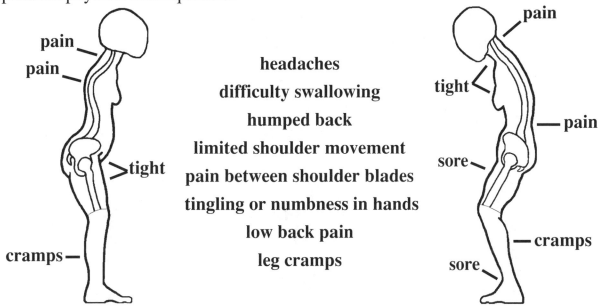

headaches
difficulty swallowing
humped back
limited shoulder movement
pain between shoulder blades
tingling or numbness in hands
low back pain
leg cramps

Hey, This Is Really Depressing, No Wonder I'm A Wreck!

Right. And small wonder that so many people go around with minor and major aches and pains. Fortunately, even the most outrageously unhealthy postures can be changed. The first step is to recognize them for what they are—habits. The second step is to begin to alter the way you do things; break the habits. Change how you sleep, shift your child to the other hip, put a cushion behind you in the chair, make yourself smile when you feel your body slumping, do whatever is the opposite of what you "usually" do. The third step is to use the exercises in this book to help stretch and strengthen your body in an even and balanced way.

Paying Attention To Yourself

This is often the hardest thing for new mothers (or fathers) to do, but it's easily the most important. You may need to stick a note up to remind yourself to stop and be aware of your body (the changing table is a good spot). Take a deep breath, relax for just a moment and take stock of your physical being. Are you slumped over? Are you standing mostly on one leg? Has it been a while since you had a drink of water?

> **TIP: If you carry a shoulder bag, is it always on the same shoulder?
> Try changing sides each time you carry it.**

Two Wrongs Can Make A Right

Look at the pictures below. If you try standing in one exaggerated bad posture and then shift your body completely to the other, something interesting happens. Try going back and forth a couple of times and then do it once very slowly. Somewhere between the two bad postures you'll find yourself standing comfortably and well.

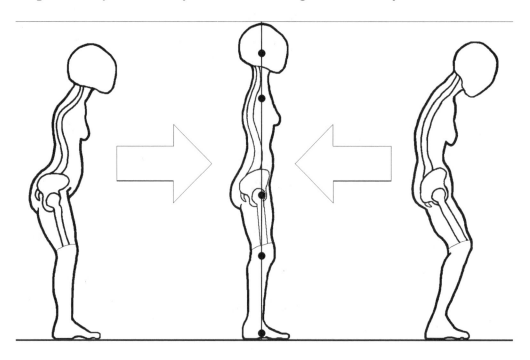

Look closely at the center figure. This is the most relaxed way to stand. Body easy. Eyes looking forward on the level. Weight comfortably balanced over the center of your arches. If you could drop a line from head to foot, it would connect your ears, shoulders, hips, backs of knees, and ankles. When your body is balanced with one part resting over another, your muscles don't have to work overtime to keep you from falling backward or forward.

TIP: If you stand for a long time (when washing dishes, for example), rest one foot on a low box or a phone book for a while. This helps the curve in the lower back and will be restful instead of stressful.

Sleeping

How To Rest Well

New mothers just don't get enough rest, although nobody needs it more! Not only is your body recuperating from the work of pregnancy and birth, but you are suddenly responsible for a new human being—one who probably hasn't gotten the sleep business figured out yet. Since you aren't going to get enough rest, how you rest (when you can) is very important.

The best way to give your body a good rest is to find a position which preserves the natural curves of your spine. Resting well when you sleep usually means lying with some support under your curves. If you lie on your back, try a towel or soft pillow under the lumbar region, add a rolled up towel to the part of your pillow that lies under your neck, and stick a big pillow under your knees. If you sleep on your side, a pillow between your legs and good support for your head will feel great.

If you sleep on your stomach - stop! It puts an enormous strain on the lower back and neck and causes many problems. The later stages of pregnancy prevented you from sleeping this way, and you should continue to avoid it. Adding a pillow, bolster, or full-sized body pillow that you can hug up close or slide between your knees will make sleeping on your side much more comfortable.

What You Sleep On

Little changes often make a big difference. Your mattress, even if it starts out as just right for you, will develop lumps, sags, and valleys from your customary sleeping positions. Regularly flip it over from side to side and from front to back.

 Many stiff necks can be avoided by using pillows that allow you to lie without your neck twisted awkwardly.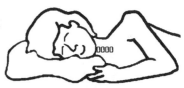

If you sleep on your back, your pillow should be soft or small enough so that your chin isn't forced forward onto your chest. This is also true for reading in bed.

Getting Out of Bed

Night feedings, cries of distress, or your own worries can bring you bolt upright in the middle of the night. However, snapping up into a sitting position from lying down, particularly when your abdominal muscles are stretched and weakened, puts a tremendous strain on the muscles of the lower back. It can cause muscle spasms and lots of discomfort.

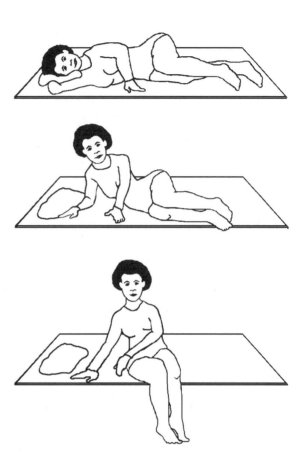

There is a safe and gentle way to rise out of bed.

First, pull in your lower belly and roll onto your side. Then push yourself upright using the strength of your arms. Bring your feet to the floor. Then stand. It doesn't take any longer and it will save you from trouble and ache.

Sleep Problems

If either you or your baby have trouble falling asleep, there is a simple technique that often works for either or both parent and child. Lie down holding your baby (either beside you or lying on top of you). Pay close attention to your infant's breath. Begin to breathe in rhythm. A baby's breath rate is much faster than yours, so begin to inhale together with your baby, but then keep slowly inhaling while the baby exhales and inhales again, then exale together. Continue to gently breathe at this rate of two to one. As you breathe along, your child will begin to relax, or give a little shudder and then relax. And you'll to relax, too. This technique also works with sick children or with a child whose crying has become hysterical.

Nap!

In the early days with your baby, resist the urge to put the house right, catch up on phone calls, and tend to everything the moment he or she is asleep. If you can, when your baby naps, nap yourself. You do need the sleep. This is just as true for adoptive parents. The new life in your house requires enormous attention. It's exhausting.

Stretching

Why Stretch?

Have you ever stood in the checkout line at the local supermarket staring at the covers of slick magazines with those incredibly fit, beautifully dressed, supple young folks and then looked around you? Was anybody like that standing in line nearby? Probably not. Most likely you saw slumped over, weary people with smeared makeup, five o'clock shadows, and small patches of dried baby food stuck here and there. In short, a lot of parents.

Those people on the magazine covers take their exercising seriously. Parents, particularly in the early months, are more likely to want to flake out, drop out, or sack out than work out. And if you're not working out, why stretch?

You need to stretch because, of course, you are working out. Nobody works out harder than the parents of small children. And nobody will profit more from a few stretches. Stretching balances out the pull of muscles on your bones and counters the tense bent over positions you get into during the day. Stretching soothes and relaxes you and protects you from muscular injuries. And most simple stretches can be done anywhere and anytime.

Strength and Flexibility, Equal Partners

We live in a society that glorifies strength and ignores flexibility. The truth is that both are equally important. The major muscle groups in our bodies all work in pairs. When one set tightens, the opposing set loosens. For our bodies to function well, both aspects, tightening and loosening, need attention.

"Muscle bound" is a phrase that has real meaning because muscles built for strength alone can wind up constricting movement and leave you vulnerable to injury unless you also learn to stretch and gain flexibility. Most of us don't work at body building. However, simply because of the way we do ordinary tasks, we develop and work certain groups of muscles much more than others. At the same time, most of us pay no attention at all to how supple we are - or aren't!

> **TIP: The most relaxing stretch of all is to lie on your back, smile, and breathe. Breathe all the way in. Let your belly rise, your ribs expand, and your shoulders rise up as you inhale; then, just as completely, relax and let it all out. If a yawn comes, yawn deeply and enjoy it.**

Muscle Talk

When you talk about muscles, the words "extensor" and "flexors" or "abductors" and "adductors" turn up from time to time. These names refer to the pairs of muscles that do the major moving for your body.

Flexors and Extensors

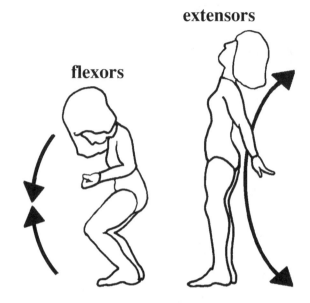

The flexor muscles generally lift things up, move them forward, or fold you over. They are often the muscles on the hairless sides of your body like the inside of the forearms and the inside backs of your knees.

The extensor muscles bring body parts back and down and straighten you up. You'll find them in the backs of your arms, your back, and in your buttocks.

Your upper arm is a good example. The biceps at the front is the flexor muscle. It curls your arm in. The triceps at the back is the extensor muscle. It bends your arm back and straightens it out.

Abductors and Adductors

There is a second set of opposing muscles in your body. These are the adductors and the abductors.

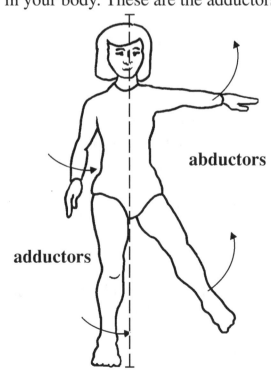

ABDUCTors take things away from the middle. Think of the word "abduction," if you want to remember the name. (The health club "Abs" are the abdominals.) The abductors are on the outside of your arms and thighs.

The **ADD**uctors bring things back towards the middle. Think of "adding." They are on the inside of arms and thighs,

Abductors and aductors work together in the same way as extensors and flexors. As one of the pair contracts, the other loosens and lengthens.

What Happens When You Stretch

When you stretch a muscle well, the muscle and the connecting tissues lengthen. When you contract a muscle, it shortens and strengthens. Health, for a muscle, is a balance between stretched and strengthened, between long and short. Correcting some conditions requires more of one than the other. When you are post-partum your abdominal muscles are over stretched and they need to be strengthened. Most of the time stretches are necessary to balance muscles that have become too taut from over use. The taut muscles of the upper chest are the balance mates of the overstretched and weakened upper back muscles that contribute to back and neck pain.

When To Stretch

For most of the stretches in this book, you won't need lots of time. A few moments of loosening up after exertion or after a long period of being in one position (like nursing) will be all you need to protect yourself. Longer sessions will help relieve built up muscle tension, correct muscle imbalances, and increase your suppleness.

Good times to stretch are early in the morning (start yourself gently, though) and before going to sleep. In the evening after a warm, relaxing bath or shower is a great time. In cold weather, make sure you're warm before beginning.

How To Stretch

Relax: Let yourself slowly enjoy the stretch. Forcing, straining, or bouncing your muscles and ligaments will do more harm than good.

Start From Where You Are: Don't compare yourself with others. Start from where you are right now and go forward.

Stretch Often: Take lots of little stretch breaks. You don't have to put on a lycra body leotard and low impact aerobic exercise shoes. Just take a moment to counteract a tightness. For example, before starting the dishes stretch your hands over your head and gently arch your back.

Smile: Don't do stretches in haste or when angry. Take the time to just sit or lie still before beginning. Imagine a cloud, blue sky, or anything else that will shift your attention from hassles and issues. Then begin to stretch.

Breathe: Be aware of your breathing as you stretch. If you catch yourself holding your breath, let it out. Breathe easily and naturally.

Be gentle with yourself: Your goal is to recover from a year or so of extreme effort and to help your body adjust to parenting's very real physical demands. Stretch lightly and gently. Pain is no gain for a parent.

An Example

You may find that your hamstrings (the muscles that run up the backs of your legs) have become tight over the last few months of your pregnancy and the early post-partum period, or they may have been tight to begin with. It's important for the health, strength, and safety of your lower back that your hamstrings be flexible, so your goal should be to stretch them out.

The "traditional" image of stretching hamstrings is touching your toes. Many people either despair of ever getting beyond their knees and give up, or they force themselves over and wind up in pain from overstretching the middle and upper back. Your goal is to stretch your hamstrings, not to touch your toes, and forcing yourself won't help you at all.

So, if you're tight, only bend forward until you can feel the stretch begin. That gentle lumbar curve is there for a reason, keep it while you stretch your hamstrings. You can use a chair, the stairs, a window sill, or the edge of a sink to support yourself. Once you are in a comfortable position and can feel the stretch begin, imagine sticking your buttocks out. This will help keep your lumbar curve. Gentle stretching will lengthen your hamstrings and protect your back.

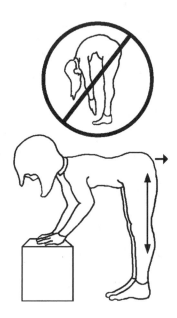

Workplace Stretching

It isn't always easy to make time at work to stretch. If more employers realized how much better work people do and how much less time they spend recovering from injuries when they can stretch out, this wouldn't be the case.

Standing up and moving around once an hour, just bending backward a little, or shaking out your wrists all help because they break up the frozen postures we get into at work. If you work at a keyboard or at something that forces you to hunch forward, roll your shoulders back and bring your shoulder blades back frequently.

TIP: Treat your body like a friend; remember it often.

Sneezing
(ahhh...choo!)

A sneeze is the sudden, involuntary expulsion of air caused by the rapid compression of the air space in your chest cavity. A lot of muscles contribute to this. The most important ones are the diaphragm and the abdominal muscles. As you inhale, the diaphragm contracts and draws down and the abdominals relax. As you exhale, the diaphragm relaxes upwards and the abdominals contract. When you sneeze (or cough), this happens fast.

Your diaphragm is a sheet of muscle and tendon that separates the contents of your chest from the contents of your belly. It attaches at the back to your lumbar spine and arches up and fans out to the lower six ribs. It works closely with your abdominal muscles and with the major back muscles.

When these muscles go into the powerful reflex action of a cough or sneeze, they place a strain on your mid and lower back. If you have a back injury or if you are under a lot of physical or emotional stress (and what parent isn't), you can pull bones out of alignment or strain muscles. You are also vulnerable if you are experiencing the hormonal changes of the child bearing year or you are having your period.

Don't worry though, it's possible to sneeze and cough safely. The trick is to relax.

- When you feel the urge to sneeze, go slightly limp and let your knees relax. If you're sitting, rest your hands on your lap and relax your whole body except the muscles of your lower belly (everything from the navel down). Tighten these and pull up on your pelvic floor (to avoid leaking urine). You can use your hands to hold and support your ribs just below your breasts.

- Do the same for a cough. If you're holding something, put it down.

- Here's how to get a second to relax yourself when you feel a sneeze or cough coming. For a sneeze, press hard at the base of your nose between your nostrils. For a cough, press at the base of your throat. This will gain you just enough time to relax and tighten the lower belly and pelvic floor.

- When you're through, don't snap back upright. Come back up slowly and take a deep, relaxed breath. Run your fingers firmly down along the bottom edge of your rib cage from the middle and out to the sides. Rub your belly just above the navel. This will help relax the muscles.

The Whole Spine
(and nothing but the spine)

About Your Spine

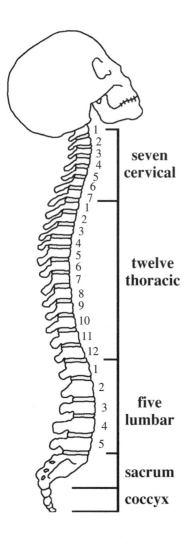

seven
cervical

twelve
thoracic

five
lumbar

sacrum

coccyx

The spine is made up of twenty-four small bones (the vertebrae), the sacrum and the coccyx.

Your spine is a wonderful example of how well your body is suited to its tasks. Each vertebra is constructed to protect the spinal cord within in it and to support the muscles that hold you together and keep you moving.

Your spine is tapered. It tapers up from the five wide lumbar vertebrae to the twelve thoracic vertebrae (they support your ribs) to the seven smaller vertebrae of the neck. The thick base supports the weight of your upper body and the thinner upper region allows the wider and more delicate motions of your head.

Your spine is curved. If you begin at the tip of your tailbone and trace the flow of the spine upwards, you will find two 'S' curves. These curves work like giant springs which protect against the jolts and shocks of life.

Your sacrum is a set of five vertebrae fused together into one scoop–shaped bone. The coccyx is a set of three tiny, fused bones. It continues the curve of the sacrum.

The spinal curves are essential for a healthy back. It's important to maintain them when sitting, standing, and even lying down. Losing the curves can cause muscle strain, soreness, and pain.

The vertebrae are separated by tough, shock absorbing sacks called discs. These are filled with a gel-like cartilage, and they cushion you from bumps and the friction of turning and bending. A balance of rest and exercise will keep your discs healthy for a life time.

As you age, the discs that separate and cushion the vertebrae in your spine slowly change. The gel-like substance is quite fluid in younger people. The gel thickens during the middle years and finally becomes fibrous and contracted in old age. This is why each age has its own characteristic disc problems. People in their middle years tend to have herniated discs where the fluid distorts weakened tissue and pushes the discs out of shape, while older people have problems with discs that shrink leaving the bones to rub together and causing arthritic conditions.

Although aging and the stresses of life slowly wear on your spinal column, there is a lot you can do to protect it while keeping yourself injury and pain free. Even after an injury, proper care, rest, and careful exercise will restore you.

The Importance of Balancing (Everything)

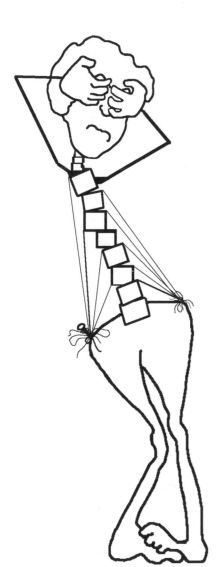

Balancing children and work, checkbooks, diets, and demands—parents have to be world class jugglers. But the most important balancing involves your body.

Imagine your spine as a column of building blocks piled one on top of the other.

If the blocks stick out every which way and are about to tip, a lot of work is required to keep them from falling over. If the blocks are well balanced and carefully placed, you stand easily.

An intricate set of muscles supports your spine. When balanced, the muscles are in harmony and you stand and work easily. When they are unbalanced, these muscles have to work extra hard to keep you from falling over and, of course, they ache.

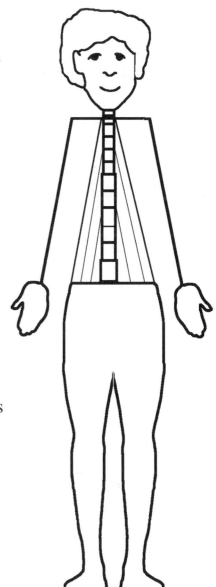

Rest and Exercise, Another Balance

The two most important things you can do for your spine seem to be contradictory. The first is to get lots of good exercise, the second is to get lots of good rest.

All day long gravity, work, chores, and children pull us down, slowly compressing our discs and squashing our vertebrae together. We all end up at the end of the day ¼ to ½ inch shorter than when we started out in the morning!

This isn't as awful as it sounds. When we lie down and rest, our discs slowly reabsorb fluid and expand. The alternation of compression and expansion is one way in which your discs and your bones get what they need to stay healthy. Nutrient fluids work their way in with the alternating pressure and release. When you rest the muscles, the tendons and ligaments attaching them to the bones return to the best position for their proper functioning.

A LAST WORD

Even if you haven't injured your back, the thought of doing nothing but rest probably seems like a great idea, but twenty-four hours of straight rest is almost as bad for you as staying up for twenty-four hours. A balance between rest and activity is as important as the balance between left and right, and front and back. Our bodies need weight bearing activity and the force of gravity to stimulate growth, nourish the bones, and maintain healthy muscle. If you are told to go to bed for two weeks after a muscular injury, perhaps you should get a second opinion.

It's not hard to learn some simple ideas, techniques, and exercises to help you balance your activities and muscles so that you can move, work, parent, and play freely. The exercises and stretches in the following chapters will help you heal from muscular injuries and keep you safe and healthy.

> **CAUTION: This book is intended to act as a guide for your well being. It is not intended to diagnose or prescribe for medical problems. If you experience inexplicable or incapacitating discomfort or have a severe injury, seek help from your health care practitioner immediately.**

The Abdominal Muscles
(don't let it all hang out!)

The Flab Blues

During the first weeks post-partum, sag and flab can get you down. You probably want to cover your belly with a big shirt and forget it. Please don't! Your abdominal muscles are the second most important set of muscles in your body to work on after the birth, after the muscles of your pelvic floor. (This is true for both vaginal and cesarean births.) For nine months these muscles have stretched farther and farther to accommodate your growing baby. Unfortunately, muscles that stretch for a long time become weakened and sag.

It can be discouraging to shed the extra weight of pregnancy and still not be able to get into your pre-baby pants. It can be even more discouraging if you develop back problems because of weak stomach muscles. You can do something about it.

Firm Is Good, Firm Is Possible

Firm abdominal muscles do more than just make you look good. They support the organs (particularly your uterus, bladder, and rectum) and soft tissue of the lower body, they protect and balance the muscles of the lower back, and they hold your body in alignment whenever you use your arms and legs.

You can restore your abdominal muscles. It will take time and concentration in the beginning and it's worth every minute. Begin slowly and work at your own pace to recover strength and tone. Some women experience a muscle separation along the mid-line of the belly which only slowly comes back together after the birth. An even smaller number may develop a hernia. Both of these conditions require caution. You will find explanations and simple tests for both in this chapter.

Hours of traditional types of abdominal exercises will do wonders for the upper belly, but nothing for the lower belly. The exercises in this chapter will help you work on both. Strong abdominal muscles, particularly in the lower belly, are essential for remaining injury free and looking and feeling your best.

CAUTION: If you had a cesarean section, read the Cesarean Section chapter beginning on page 6 before trying any abdominal exercises.

Two Important Self Tests

Before you begin any post-partum exercise program for your abdominals you should make two simple tests. They will help you check the health and tone of these muscles. You are looking for two things, first, for the amount of separation in your abdominal muscles, and second, for any possible hernia.

Hormonal changes affect your abdominal muscles. Some hormones that you produce during pregnancy will loosen the connective tissues in your body to make gestation and birth possible. The abdominal muscles come together along a band of this tissue which runs from the bottom of your rib cage down to the top of your pubic bone. It's called the linea alba. In its loose, separated state, it doesn't anchor your abdominal muscles as well as it once did and won't for a while after the birth.

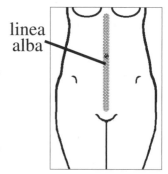

linea alba

Some separation is normal, but a large separation means that you will have to use caution. If you suspect you have either of these conditions, don't do these exercises until you have checked with your medical practitioner or a physical therapist.

CAUTION: It can be dangerous to act on self-diagnosis. These tests are to alert you to possible medical problems. If you suspect a condition that requires medical attention, please consult your health care practitioner.

A Test For Separation (diastasis recti)

Diastasis Recti is the medical term for the separation that occurs in the abdominal muscles during pregnancy. It is completely normal. The muscles naturally spread apart to accommodate your growing child. The separation starts small and widens during the pregnancy. After the birth, the process reverses and eventually your abdominal muscles return to normal.

Some separations are very wide, and women with this condition need to take extra care while rehabilitating their abdominal muscles. A separation is usually measured in finger widths. One to two finger widths is considered normal, but a separartion of two and a half to three finger widths usually requires some kind of intervention to protect the abdominal muscles. If you have a wide separation use extreme caution when you are exercising and exercise only after having a medical evaluation. This is not an incapacitating condition, but it does require care.

Checking Yourself

Here's how to measure the amount of separation in your abdominal muscles:

Lie on your back. Bring your knees up with your feet on the floor. Relax and take a couple of gentle breaths.

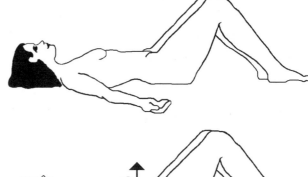

Breathe in. Let your belly expand. Feel for the gully between the bands of muscle that run down the center of your belly.

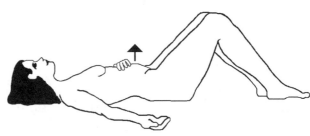

Breathe out, pull your belly in, and do a partial sit-up (bring head and shoulders up only, the lower part of your shoulder blades should still touch the floor).

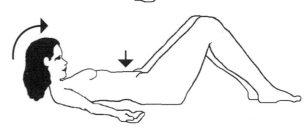

Slide your fingers back into the gully around the navel. The deeper gully you will now feel is the diastasis.

Stick your fingers straight down into the gully (about to the depth of the first knuckle) so that they fill it. Feel the muscles on either side. The number of fingers in the gully between the muscles is the width of the diastasis.

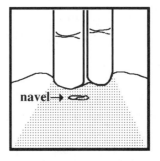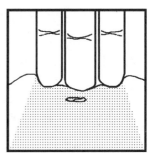

navel →

NORMAL   **CAUTION**

A partial sit-up positon is used to check this condition so that each time you check yourself, you can do it accurately.

CAUTION: With a separation, don't do sit ups or exercises that make you hold your breath or bear down on your bladder, uterus, or rectum.

A Test For Abdominal Hernia

Abdominal hernias are not common and, if you have one, you've probably noticed it already. To be safe, however, try this test on yourself before beginning any exercise program. A hernia in the muscles that support the abdominal cavity can be serious. Straining or over exercising with this condition risks pulling or tearing the muscles away from their attachments. The bulge may accompany a wide separation, but it can also appear in women with a only a mild diastasis.

Checking Yourself

Lie on your back. Bring your knees up while keeping your feet on the floor.

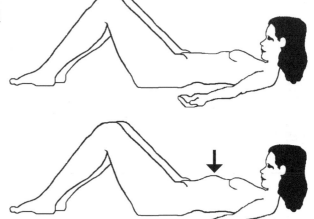

Bring your head and shoulders up and look at your belly.

If you see a prominent bulge running down the center of your belly (it's often between the rib cage and the navel), you may have a hernia.

Although this is not a terribly serious condition, you should have a medical evaluation. Women with a hernia need to be very careful during pregnancy and in the post-partum period. Exercising, heavy lifting, and incorrectly getting up from a lying down position (always roll to your side first), can make it much harder to rehabilitate your abdominal muscles later on.

Severe cases requiring surgery are very rare. For most women, a few simple techniques will protect the stomach muscles. Learning to lift correctly, learning to roll to the side and use your arms when getting up from a lying position, and not straining on the toilet should be enough. Your health care practitioner may suggest you use an abdominal binder for a while after the birth. In all cases, avoid strenuous exercise programs, particularly sit ups, until this condition is corrected.

> **CAUTION: If you suspect you have a wide separation or a bulge in your abdominal muscles, get an evaluation from your health care provider.**

There's no way to avoid what happens to your abdominal muscles in pregnancy. Pregnancy stretches them for so long that sagging almost seems natural. Then comes the hard work of labor! The stress of labor and the overstretching make it very important to rehabilitate and re-educate your abdominals. Fortunately, there are many things you can do soon after your baby is born. In fact, if you regularly use the exercises in this section, your belly will wind up in better shape than before.

Most people find it easy to isolate and contract the "Popeye" muscle in the upper arm, the biceps. It's almost as easy to isolate and contract the abdominal muscles. If you suck your stomach in, you're using them. Try it. The next step is to suck in the belly above your navel and then your belly below the navel (without holding your breath). The lower abdominals are the more important. They support and protect your back while lifting and they support and protect your internal organs. Begin with...

The Basic Breath

Lie down on your back and let your arms sprawl out to the sides. Bring your knees up by sliding your feet toward your buttocks. Inhale and exhale a few times.

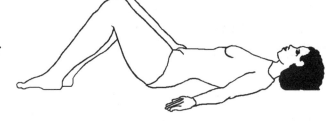

Don't flatten your back along the floor by tilting your pelvis. Let the natural, relaxed curve remain. Breathe in slowly and deeply. The belly rises and expands.

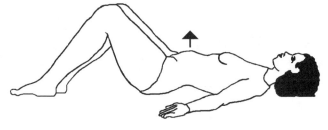

Breathe out. The belly sinks, the muscles contract. Imagine pulling your navel back toward your spine. Repeat this cycle several times. Remember to tighten the muscles below the navel and don't flatten your lower back.

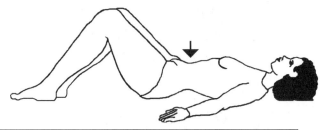

> **CAUTION: No heroics, please!** If you had a cesarean, a wide separation, hernia, or experience any increase in bleeding, consult with your health care provider before you do any abdominal exercises.

Sahrmann's Exercises

Shirley Sahrmann is a physical therapist who has thought long and hard about the problems of strengthening and rehabilitating the abdominal muscles. She has designed an excellent series of exercises. As with all the other exercises in this book, begin slowly, work gently, and don't push through pain. If something starts to hurt, stop, figure out why it hurts, and work at a more comfortable pace. You can also consult with someone who will modify the exercise for you. In the beginning, work slowly and master the exercise correctly. Later you can work harder.

First Step

Lie on the floor knees up and arms out to the sides.

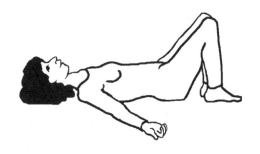

Hold your belly in by tightening your lower abdominal muscles. Take some small breaths with your upper chest (a "trumpet" breath works best, breathe in and then blow out through your lips as if you were blowing a trumpet or making a "raspberry" sound).

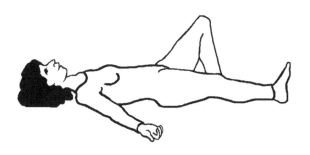

Keep the belly tight and pulled in while you slide one leg down along the floor until it lies flat. Slide your leg back up to a bent position. Relax your belly. Repeat the same process for the leg on the other side. Don't flatten your back out on the floor, keep your normal relaxed curve.

Keeping the lower abdominal muscles tight holds your pelvis steady and maintains that stability while your legs work. When your abdominals work, your back muscles don't (and they don't get strained). This exercise trains your abdominal muscles to do just what they are supposed to do.

> **TIP: Keep the natural curve in your lower back, don't flatten it out for these particular exercises. If your pelvic floor seems weaker or if you have stress incontinence, you are pushing yourself too hard. Back up one step. Do more repetitions at that level until your are stronger.**

Second Step

When you can do twenty leg slides on each side, you can move on to this step. Now you'll raise each leg toward your chest and extend it out above the floor.

Pull your belly in and hold it while you raise one leg toward your chest.

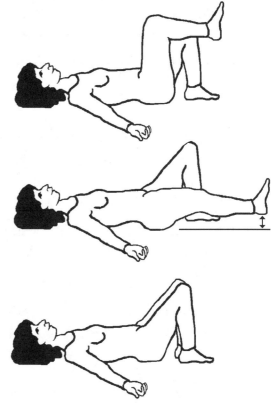

Extend the leg straight out parallel to the floor, but without touching it.

Finally, return the leg to its beginning position with your foot on the floor and relax your belly. Do the same for the other leg. After you've done this once for each leg, do it five times on each side without pausing.

Third Step

When you can do twenty times on each side without discomfort (and without your back arching too far off the floor), you are ready to try both legs. For the second step your abdominals were lifting up the equivalent of 10 to 12 pounds. In this one you will be holding up 20 to 25 pounds.

Breathe in, then breathe out and pull your belly in. Raise one leg toward your chest. With your belly still pulled in, bring the other leg up.

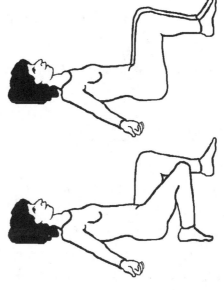

Touch the first leg back down to the floor and then raise it up again. Lower the second leg to the floor and raise it up. Repeat this cycle ten times.

Fourth Step

Keep your belly sucked in and extend one leg out while keeping the other up in the air. Then bring your leg back up and extend the other one. Repeat this cycle so that each leg is extended ten times.

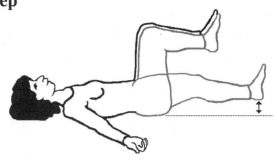

Fifth Step

Don't attempt this until you are able to do the previous step twenty times for each leg without your belly bulging or your back arching.

Bring both legs up to your chest, one at a time. Remember to keep your lower abdominals tight and your lower back flat.

Straighten both legs up toward the ceiling. Keep your legs together and slowly lower them back toward the floor.

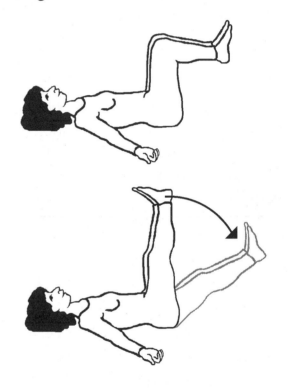

As soon as you feel your back begin to arch or your belly begin to bulge, bring your legs back up. Then slowly lower again. Your goal should be twenty times.

To rest, bend your legs at the knees again and then lower your legs, one at a time.

If you feel your hip click, don't lower your legs as far. What you sense is probably just a tendon sliding over the hip bone, but it's better to be cautious. The goal is to build abdominal strength without hurting yourself.

Advanced Exercises

You've seen those ads with slim young women getting even slimmer with rubber bands, pulley systems, or rock-a-boards. They promise to flatten your stomach and, surprise, they do work. Cuff or hand weights (or detergent containers!) benefit your abdominal muscles in the same way. But, and this is a big BUT, remember to use what you have learned about breathing and your lower (below the belly button) abdominals. There is a helpful stretchband floor exercise on page 123.

Sit Ups? Be Cautious.

Some exercises, sit ups in particular, can do more harm than good in the post-partum period unless you do them carefully. Sit ups are very good exercises, but only after you have developed a good foundation of strong abdominals. Work through all of the Sahrmann exercises before doing any.

Always follow this procedure for sit ups; it will help "knit" your muscles back together and make sit ups safer.

> **Sit Up Tip:**
>
> • **Breathe in, filling your belly up.**
>
> • **Exhale (use the "trumpet")**
>
> • **Pull your lower belly in and hold it in.**
>
> • **Then do the sit-up.**

Here's why.

Imagine your hands lying on your belly. When your muscles pop out to pull you up to sitting, it's as if your hands were clenching into fists. You can see how your fingers are pulled away from the center line. This increases the stretch and sag.

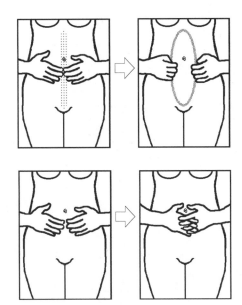

Now imagine your hands lying open across your belly again. If you pull your belly in, the fingers slide toward the center. The tips knit together. This helps hold the separation together when you contract the muscles and come up to a sitting position.

> **CAUTION:** Sit ups are a dangerous way to begin restoring your abdominal muscles. They put too much strain on the lower back and create too great a risk for increasing any abdominal separation.

Abdominal Binders

An abdominal binder is a corset-like support that wraps around your middle. Its purpose is to hold your stomach muscles in and support them. Some women who have carried large babies find their abdominal muscles extremely stretched. The more the muscles are stretched, the weaker they become and the harder they are to restore.

If you need an abdominal binder, you'll find that it increases your comfort during exercise and prevents the muscles from becoming more stretched while standing, working out, taking long walks, or jogging. By reducing sagging and stretching, it can also speed recovery.

These belts or corsets should only be used until the muscles are strong enough to support themselves. You can try wearing it less and less as each day goes on while you rehabilitate your abdominal muscles.

A variety of abdominal binders are available through pharmacies and medical supply stores. They range in price from $20 to $150 and even the least expensive can help a lot. Your health care practitioner can help you decide which model is best for your particular needs.

• LIFTING NOTE •

Use the same breathing technique for lifting that you do for exercising the lower abdominal muscles. Most people unconsciously hold their breath when lifting something heavy. Holding your breath puts unnecessary strain on the pelvic floor muscles, sometimes causes stress incontinence, and strains the abdominal muscles. To avoid this...

- **Pull your belly in and pull the pelvic floor muscles up.**

- **Then, as you start to lift, begin to exhale.**

- **Continue to exhale and lift.**

Following these steps will protect your lower back, pelvic floor, and abdominal muscles. This is so important that you should write these steps on a piece of paper and stick it up wherever you do a lot of lifting. On the wall behind your changing table would be a good place.

TIP: Lifting properly will become second nature with practice. It will help you avoid urinary stress incontinence, slim your belly, and protect your lower back. It means less work for you and less discomfort.

A Last Word

Most of us have the habit of using what is called the 'Val Salva Maneuver' when tightening the abdominals. The Val Salva Maneuver is when you close your mouth, hold your breath, and bear down. We use this during bowel movements and, unconsciously and unfortunately, we use it when we lift.

The Val Salva puts enormous pressure on the uterus, the bladder, and the pelvic floor muscles. Many later pelvic floor problems can be prevented by learning and using the "basic breath" technique. If you pull in the lower abdominal muscles and exhale while you lift (or push), you will create much less pressure and strain on the pelvic floor muscles and you will get just as much done.

Use the basic breath when you have a bowel movement and when you urinate. Try to avoid straining at either.

Unlearning the Val Salva is particularly important if you plan to become pregnant again. Your labor will be easier and your pelvic floor structure will be safer when the basic breath becomes a basic habit.

A Look Inside: The Abdominal Muscles

Three sets of strong muscle layer your belly with a web of support and strength. The technical names of your muscles can be confusing and hard to remember, but three are important and distinct enough to label.

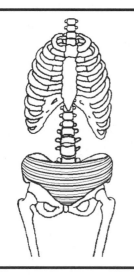 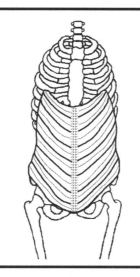 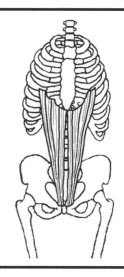

transversus	**obliques**	**rectus abdominus**
The transversus stretches from side to side across your lower belly. It tightens when you have a bowel movement and it supports your lower back and internal organs when you lift. This is the muscle you should pull in each time you pick something up.	The obliques criss-cross your belly from the lower ribs and the back. There are two layers to this muscle which holds the pelvis in alignment, balances your back, keeps your organs in place, and turns the upper body from side to side when the pelvis is held steady.	These muscles run up and down the front on either side of the belly button from the ribs to the pubic bone. They bend your upper body forward over the pelvis, when the pelvis is steady, or they tilt the pelvis up, if the upper body is held steady. They act as a brace for your spine, particularly when you are carrying something.

These muscles are overstretched and weakened during pregnancy. Strengthening them protects your lower back from injury, provides support for your internal organs, and will help heal your pelvic floor.

CAUTION: Hormonal changes will cause looseness in your joints and connective tissue for several months after the birth. Exercise carefully.

Just Me and My Sacroiliac
(open that gate)

COMMON PROBLEMS

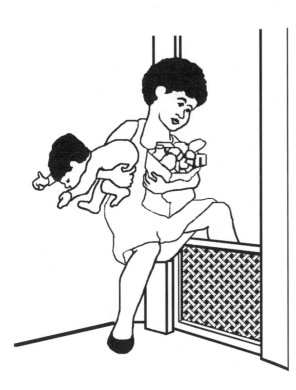

The child gate is a wonderful and very necessary piece of baby equipment. However, in our rush through the day we're always tempted to step over it, and this is a frequent cause of painful injury to the sacroiliac joint.

Stepping over the gate instead of opening it puts a tremendous strain on the ligaments that hold the sacroiliac joint together. It's easy to push the bones so far out of their normal range of motion that they catch and jam up. Considerable discomfort is the result.

Of course, people do move this way. Look at the hurdlers on a track team; they kick their legs up and over all the time. However, the hurdler has a coach, a trainer, a warm-up period, a time to stretch—and isn't carrying twenty pounds of reluctant infant and fifteen pounds of groceries.

If you have a toddler as well as a newborn, you are even more vulnerable because your body is working harder. If you are a postpartum mother recovering from the effort of birth and the hormonal loosening of your ligaments, <u>and</u> you are the mother of a toddler, you bend, lift, carry, and worry enough for an entire Olympic team. You don't need sacroiliac problems.

Yes, it does take a little extra time to open the gate. It's worth it.

CAUTION NOTE: In the post-partum period there are many hormonal changes. Your period may start and then disappear again. This will cause the ligaments of your sacroiliac to loosen and tighten irregularly. Your pelvis will be unpredictably vulnerable. Use the suggestions and exercises in this chapter—even when you think you don't need them!

Rotation

The most common sacroiliac problem occurs when one of the iliac bones gets twisted against the sacrum. This is called a rotation. One side can become twisted slightly forward or backward. If the iliac bone is twisted forward, it's called an anterior rotation; if it's twisted backward, it's a posterior rotation.

It's easy to see how it happens. Your body weight and the great strength of the leg and back muscles that attach to the sides of the pelvis create powerful forces. Hormonal changes loosen the connecting ligaments, and times of emotional stress or fatigue, or any one-sided muscular activity can apply these forces unequally and twist parts of the joint out of place.

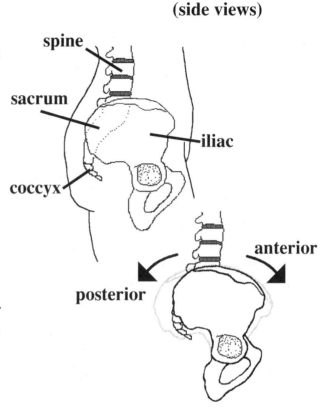

(side views)

spine

sacrum

iliac

coccyx

anterior

posterior

Possible Causes of Rotation

- standing up and turning while lifting something heavy

- missing a curb or step and landing hard on one foot

- making love with your legs far apart

- sitting on soft, squishy or very low chairs

- crossing your legs when you sit

- stepping over a child gate while carrying a load

- tight hip muscles from sitting at a desk all day

- driving in a car for long distances

> **TIP: Sacroiliac problems can sometimes be confused with vertebral disc problems. Both can stress the sciatic nerve and cause similar tingling, numbness, burning sensations, or pain down the leg. You should get a correct diagnosis from your health care practitioner because treatments for the two conditions are very different.**

Since the sacroiliac joint is held together by ligaments and not muscles, it isn't possible to do exercises that strengthen the joint itself. Keeping your sacroiliac safe and pain free is mostly a task of prevention.

You can prevent injuries in three ways: by avoiding certain actions, by doing some other things carefully, and by strengthening and balancing the muscles that indirectly affect the sacroiliac joint.

Things to avoid at all costs

- Never step over a child gate.

- Never lift and turn while rising from a squatting position.

- Avoid slumping over when sitting and avoid seats that you sink into.

- When you get out of a car don't always step out on one leg. Sometimes swivel around in your seat and put both feet on the ground first before getting out.

Things you can't avoid, but should do with care

- Driving on long trips is hard. Take frequent breaks and walk around. Slide your car seat back or forward from time to time to alter the angle of your legs.

- When you stand from a kneeling position, try to alternate the leg you put your weight on. Don't always come up on the same side.

- Try not to sit in only one position. Stand up and stretch your legs as often as you can by walking. If you cross your legs, alternate sides.

Things you should do

- The sacroiliac joint is the top of the arch that divides your weight between each leg. Balance your activities and use each side of your body equally.

- If a chair is uncomfortable, change it. Sit on a cushion that changes the angle of your leg to your pelvis or put a cushion behind you.

- Find love making positions that are comfortable and don't force your legs too far to the sides; alternate positions frequently.

- Use the exercises in this section to balance and strengthen the muscles that surround the sacroiliac as well as those that join and attach to other connecting bones. The chapter on the hip (page 98) has other helpful exercises.

Exercises and Stretches

The following exercises will strengthen, stabilize, and balance the muscles that surround the sacroiliac joint. They can sometimes correct minor problems. This doesn't always work, but trying them carefully won't harm you, and it just might do the trick. The exercises are also good for limbering up and strengthening the back and the stomach muscles that support your lumbar spine.

If you have time, take a warm bath before you begin and let yourself completely relax. You can do these exercises individually, but since you're going to be lying down anyway, you might as well do them as a series.

The Leg Roll

Lie comfortably on your back with your arms out to your sides. Bring your knees up, while keeping you feet on the floor.

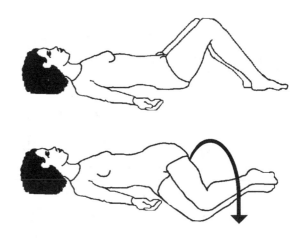

Gently roll your legs first to one side and then the other. At first keep your feet on the floor and go only as far over as is comfortable. Later, you can let your knees roll further and let them carry your feet with them.

The further you go, the more stretch for the opposite side of your lower back. Rock back and forth, side to side, and keep your stomach sucked in as you move. You can do a basic breath each time you come back to the center. It's very relaxing.

The leg roll is a stretch that balances the muscles that connect the lower back to the hip bones. If these muscles relax and you balance the left and right sides, an abnormal rotation will sometimes correct itself or a kink in your lower back may work itself out.

You can stretch different places in your lower back by changing your knee position. The tighter your knees are and the closer your feet are to your buttocks, the lower the stretch for your back. The further out that you slide your legs, the higher up the stretch on your back.

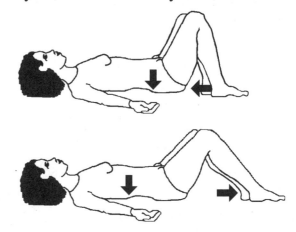

The Pelvic Tilt

Lie on your back and relax for a moment and then touch the tips of your hip bones with your finger tips. Rock your pelvis so that you can feel your hip bones rolling forward and back.

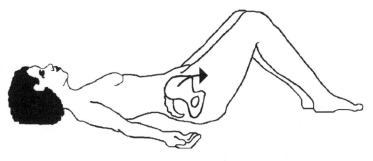

Let your hands rest to the sides with your palms up. Tip your pelvis forward, toward your feet and away from your head. You will feel your chin come forward a little, the curve in your neck flatten out, and your back arch up.

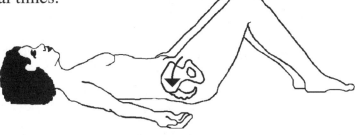

Next, rock your pelvis back toward the floor so that the crests move toward your chest. This will flatten the lumbar curve and your head will tip back a little. Repeat, back and forth, several times.

This exercise will rock you back and forth over your sacral bone. If it has become tipped too far back or too far forward, the rocking motion may put it back into place and relieve pressure that you feel across the bottom of your back or in the center of your buttocks. It's a wonderful exercise for your whole lower back.

CAUTION: High heels are unfriendly to your pelvis. They chronically shorten the hamstring muscles at the back of the legs. When these are tight, they can pull your pelvis out of alignment. If you have to wear them, make sure that you use stretches for hamstring flexibility. Change out of high heels as soon as you can and wear them as little as possible.

The Pelvic Clock

Lie on your back, relaxed, knees up and arms out to the sides. Imagine that you are lying on top of the face of a clock.

The base of your spine is on 12 o'clock and the tip of your sacrum is on 6 o'clock. The two sacro-iliac joints are on 2 o'clock and 10 o'clock. The lower edges of your buttocks are on 4 o'clock and 8 o'clock.

Do a regular back and forth pelvic tilt (12 o'clock to 6 o'clock and back).

Next, press down on 10 o'clock with the back of your right pelvic bone (the iliac).

Move your attention to the back of your left pelvic bone and push down on 2 o'clock.

Go down to the bottom of your left buttock and press it down on 4 o'clock.

Then press the bottom of your right buttock down on 8 o'clock.

Now make a full circle by working your way all around the clock. Then reverse direction and go back around the other way.

You can do this two or three times and then rest a moment. Finish with a couple of pelvic tilts (going from 12 o'clock to 6 o'clock and back again).

Using Your Muscles

If you look in the mirror and can see that the upper edges of your iliac bones are rotated and uneven, you can try this technique for getting things back into place. (If it isn't clear, you can hold a yardstick or something similar so that it touches the upper iliac edge on each side.) Then, lie on your back and bring your legs up one at a time.

When your right side is lower, **try this:**

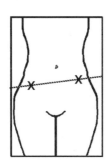

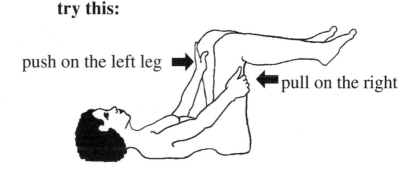

push on the left leg ➡ ⬅ pull on the right

When your left side is lower, **try this:**

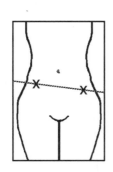

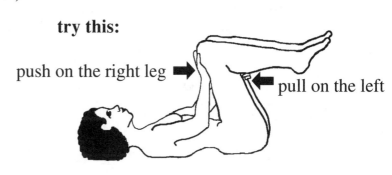

push on the right leg ➡ ⬅ pull on the left

This works because you are using your muscles to counteract the strains that pulled you out of alignment. Pushing on one leg pulls the iliac bone on that side down while pulling on the opposite leg pulls the other one up.

You can do the same thing with a friend or partner. Have him or her stand or kneel next to you while you lie on a table top or bed. Lie on the side which has the higher of the two iliac crests (the picture shows the position for right side high and left side low). Make a scissors around your partner by placing your upper leg in front of and around the waist and your lower leg behind with the knee in the hollow of the back. Then squeeze your thighs together.

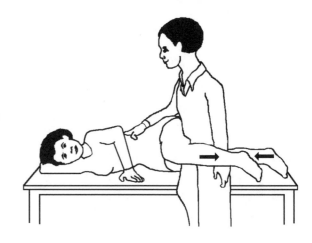

Pushing Into The Floor

This exercise is good for people who tend to have posterior rotations. It balances the muscles on both sides of the pubic bone and will help prevent problems.

Lie face down on a comfortable surface and bring your arms up to the level of your shoulders or head. Raise the lower leg on one side and push that thigh straight down into the floor, holding for a count of ten. Repeat this on the other side. Do both sides two or three times.

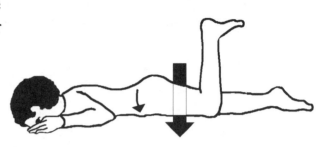

Tightenting the muscles on the front of the leg will pull the iliac bone forward and down. Sometimes this will correct the rotation.

Rotation Checks

If you can't spot the tops of the iliac bones, you can sometimes tell which side is causing you trouble by trying one of these two tests. In some cases doing either one of them may be enough to pop the misaligned joint back into place. Don't force them, however, and if you have any doubts consult with your health care practitioner.

Place the foot of the painful side on the chair seat behind you. Gently push the iliac bone forward using your hand on the back of your hip. You can also try this kneeling on the floor with the affected leg behind you.

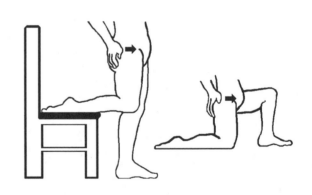

If you feel better, then the rotation may be posterior (tilted back). If you feel worse, the rotation may be anterior (tilted forward).

If that doesn't help you can try this:

Lie on the floor. Bring the knee on the affected side toward your chest. If it feels better the rotation is anterior and this position is relieving it. If it's worse, the rotation is posterior.

Massage

Any part of your body profits from the soothing and thoughtful energy of a good massage. You can do it for yourself or have a friend massage you.

Sacroiliac soreness can be helped by gently rolling a tennis ball, or a rubber ball of a similar size, over the sore spots. Lie on your side or stomach to do this. It's a little awkward to get to all the places, so having someone else do it is easier. Use only gentle pressure and put a pillow underneath your hips to support your pelvis.

There is a gentle massage that you can do for yourself. It looks like the leg roll, but your legs don't go as far.

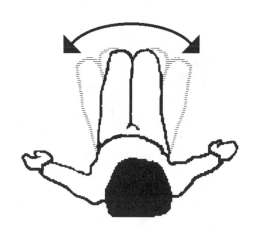

Lie on your back and draw your knees up with your feet still on the floor. Keeping your knees together, gently and slowly roll over your sacrum from side to side. It gives the sacrum a massage and will relax some of the muscles in your lower back.

CAUTION: Your sacroiliac joint can be influenced by both lumbar spinal problems and leg length imbalances. If your condition is chronic or keeps you from normal activities, have your health care practitioner make a thorough evaluation.

• LIFTING NOTE •

Safe lifting for your sacroiliac joint is simple. Don't lift and twist at the same time. The chapter Step by Step (page 34) has some good suggestions for healthy lifting. The chapter on The Changing Table (page 23) will give you some practical help with the place where you'll probably be doing a lot of lifting for the next couple of years.

A positive lifting strategy that will give you some protection is to use a wide stance. This will give you a strong base of support because the force of your weight is directed down and out through the legs. It allows you to use the strength of your legs most efficiently while you keep the natural curve in your lower back and reduce awkward pulls on your sacroiliac joint.

• NURSING NOTE •

The big threat to your sacroiliac joint while nursing is your sitting position. Avoid soft, squishy chairs, low couches, directors chairs, or any kind of sitting surface that will sag and let your knees rise above the level of your hips.

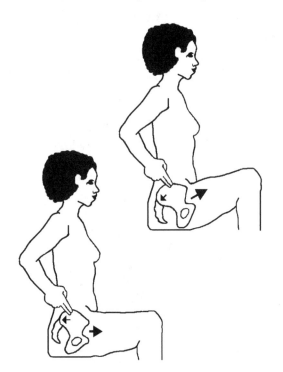

Here's why. When you sit with your knees higher than your hips, your sacroiliac joint is under extra pressure because you are rotated backward. If your ligaments are lax because of hormonal changes, if you already have soreness in this region, or if you have had previous sacroiliac problems, you are at a greater risk getting stuck in this rotation and getting up will be painful.

It's also a good idea to avoid sitting in umbrella or beanbag chairs. These compress your pelvis, make it hard to keep your knees level with your hips, and encourage the rest of you to slump.

Maintain good sitting posture while you nurse. Everyone is tempted to cross a leg to bring the baby up, but don't do it! If you need to bring your baby closer, use a pillow. Never crossing your legs above the knees will protect you from unnecessary discomfort. If you cross your legs anyway, at least make sure that you alternate sides.

If you do feel stiff and unbalanced around the hips when you get up, try a standing pelvic tilt.

Stand about three feet from a wall and lean into it with your arms. Keep your legs straight and your feet about as far apart as your hips. Gently rock your pelvis back and forth several times. This will relax the muscles and restore the balance. If one side is sore, shift your weight to that side and do some more tilts.

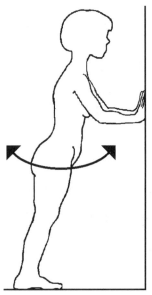

A Last Word

Look at this picture:

It shows the traditional I'm-in-a-hurry, jump in the car, getaway technique. Unless you're trying to shave seconds off your speedway record or robbing a bank, forget it. It's almost guaranteed to cause you the grief of a rotated sacroiliac joint.

It's much safer to use these two steps to get in and out of the car.

First, sit down on the car seat by backing in, knees together, and sitting yourself facing out.

Second, pivot and bring both knees in together. It's simple, just about as quick, and much safer.

If your car seat is too low or tipped too far back, your knees are pushed up higher than your hips. Use a firm cushion to raise yourself up (or tip yourself forward) so that your thighs are parallel to the floor.

> **TIP: The powerful muscles of the lower back and thighs surround your hips. They determine the health and stability of your sacroiliac joint. If you have sarcoiliac trouble, read the hip chapter (page 98) next.**

A Look Inside: The Sacroiliac Joints

Each of the two large wings of your pelvis, the iliac bones (your hip bones), join your spine at its base, the sacrum, to make the sacroiliac joints. These joints are plane joints where two relatively flat surfaces are held together by ligaments.

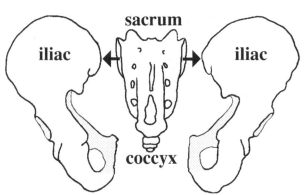

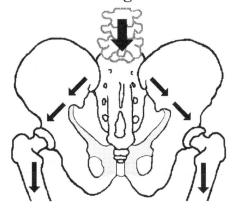

The two sacroiliac joints connect the sides of the arch that supports the whole weight of your upper body and transfers it to the hip joints and then down the legs.

Since these joints are only held together by connective tissue, no bands of working muscle run directly across them to hold then together. When these ligaments are relaxed by hormonal changes, then stress, strain, or muscle imbalance can pull the bones out of place.

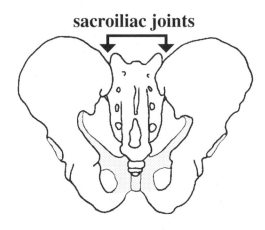

You are most vulnerable to sacroiliac injuries during the pre-natal and post-partum period and just before and after your monthly period. At these times the levels of progesterone, estrogen, prolactin, and relaxin are much greater in your body. These hormones have many benefits, one of which is to loosen the ligaments around the pelvis. This is great during childbirth, but not so great afterwards, especially if you try to straddle the child gate on your way home from the supermarket.

The Lumbar Spine
(the buck, all too often, stops here)

COMMON PROBLEMS

When people think of back pain, they often imagine an elderly person hobbling along with one hand on a cane and the other on the lower back. Many of us know that this creaking elder is frequently a creaking "younger."

Lumbar problems can echo elsewhere. Certain leg pains are caused by pressure on the nerves in the lumbar region. You may feel the pain in your buttocks, legs, or feet, but the problem is in the lower back. Sometimes pain in the lumbar region is an echo from a condition in another part of the body. Any continuing and disturbing pain in this area should be carefully evaluated by your medical practitioner.

Some Lower Back Symptoms

- Generalized pains anywhere along the spine and as far up as the neck

- Pain across the lower back

- Difficulty in straightening up after bending over

- Pain running down into buttocks

- Numbness or tingling sensation down into leg and foot

- Pain down the front or sides of the thigh or groin

Rest is always good when an injury is acute, but it isn't a miracle cure for back problems. Many people are no better off after a week of complete bed rest than before. Total rest can even make some conditions worse. You will heal yourself best with a balance of rest, stretches, corrective exercises, and daily activities.

> **TIP: Soreness or pain from a strained muscle should diminish within seven to ten days and heal within four to six weeks. If it takes longer, you should seek medical help, if you haven't already.**

A pain in the lower back is a warning. If the pain is accompanied by tingling, numbness, or extends down the legs, or if your normal activities are seriously interrupted by the pain, it is a big warning. You should have your condition evaluated. If the pain or ache is present but doesn't incapacitate you, it's a small warning to ease up, lighten up, and change the way you do things. The most important things for you to think about changing are your posture, how you lift and carry, how you sit and sleep, and your exercise program.

All post-partum mothers, whether they delivered vaginally or by cesarean, have experienced profound changes in the abdominal muscles. These muscles support your internal organs and work together with the muscles of the lower back to protect you from injuries. They are crucial for a healthy lower back. Be sure to read the chapter on the abdominal muscles on page 61, particularly if you still have muscle separation (diastasis recti) or any abdominal weakness. If you have had a cesarean, read "Recovering From Cesarean Sections" on page 6 before going any further.

Stretches and Exercises

As you do the stretches and exercises in this chapter, remember:

• As you do them, think about your breathing. Breathe in, breathe, out and pull your lower belly in as you begin any move. Don't hold your breath or suck in only the part of your belly above the navel. The muscles of the lower belly are the ones that protect your lower back.

• Your lower back has a natural curve. When you lie on your back to do a stretch, be aware of this curve. As you do the stretch, keep the curve. If you feel your back flattening to the floor or arching up, you are pushing yourself too hard.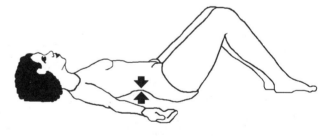

• Do all of the stretches and exercises gently and carefully. The goal is to help your body recover while slowly building strength and flexibility.

> **TIP: Notice if one side of your back feels tighter than the other. Do you habitually carry your baby, your groceries, or your purse on that side? Alternating sides when you carry will strengthen and stretch both sides of your body instead of straining one.**

The Child Pose

This is one of the most basic, useful, and relaxing of the traditional yoga poses. It gives you a gentle and general overall stretch for the back.

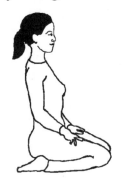  

Kneel on a soft surface. Breathe in deeply and exhale. As you exhale...

Place your hands beside your knees and gently lower yourself until your chest rests on your thighs and your forehead rests on the ground.

Slide your arms around to the sides and behind you. Breath slowly and deeply. Let your body relax.

When you come up, place your hands beside your knees and push up with your arms. Make sure you tighten your lower abdominal muscles as you push up.

Modified Child Pose

If you have back pain, or are too stiff to get all the way down, you will find that modifying the stretch with a support will give you the same benefits. It will also relax tension and beginning back muscle spasms.

Use several firm cushions to support the upper body. Imagine your tailbone tilting down and dropping away.

If you are a little looser, lay one hand on top of the other in front of your knees and rest your forehead on them.

People who are stiff in the knees or ankles can still use this stretch by placing a firm pillow under their thighs as well or by resting the upper body on a chair, couch, or pile of cushions.

Abdominal Exercises

Probably the most important set of muscles for protecting your lower back are those in your lower belly. Your next step should be to learn the Sahrmann exercises on page 66 in the chapter on the abdominal muscles, if you haven't already. Once you have mastered them, you can move on to the knee to chest exercise.

Knee to Chest Stretch

In this stretch it is very important to tighten the lower abdominals as you bring your legs up. This strengthens the abdominal muscles, stretches the muscles of the lumbar spine, and protects the lower back

Begin by lying on your back and relaxing with a few basic breaths.

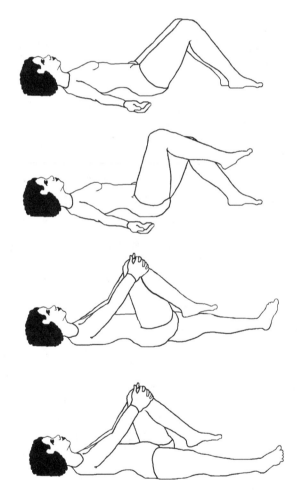

Exhale, and as your lower belly tightens and pulls in, slide your knees up, while keeping your feet in contact with the floor.

Slowly raise one knee toward your chest. Keep your belly in and don't let your back arch up or flatten more than its natural curve.

Catch your knee with both hands and gently draw it toward your chin. Your other leg stays straight out on the floor.

Lower your leg back to the floor and do the same with your other leg. Repeat five times on each side.

After you've done both legs a couple of times, see if you feel tighter on one side or the other. Repeat the stretch on the tight side and hold it a little longer. Imagine drawing your breath into that side and making it softer and longer.

Knee to Forehead

When you can bring your knees up easily on each side, and your back feels loose enough, then you can move on to this second step.

Support your neck with one hand. Draw one knee up while raising your head to meet it. Bring your knee toward your forehead and touch it if you can.

Remember to exhale as you bring your knee up. Stretch each side 5 times.

Pelvic Tilt

This is an exercise for the sacroiliac joint. We're repeating it here because it is an excellent way to wind down from doing the knee to chin exercise which works one side and then the other. The pelvic tilt irons out the differences. You'll find this exercise in greater detail on page 77.

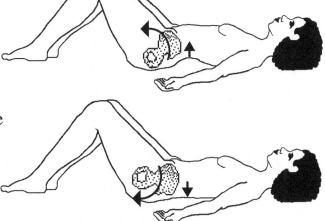

Tip your pelvis forward, toward your feet and away from your head. You will feel your chin come forward a little, the curve in your neck flatten out, and your back arch up.

Next, rock your pelvis back toward the floor so that the crests move toward your chest. This will flatten the lumbar curve and your head will tip back a little. Rock back and forth several times.

The pelvic tilt is not a cure for low back pain. It's a useful exercise and stretch, but it can cause you more grief, if you use it when you are having muscles spasms.

Bending Backward

Like the rest of your spine, the lumbar region suffers from all the hunched over things we do. When you bend forward all the time, some of the bones begin to shift and you risk developing a chronic posture with your back humped over, your head thrust forward, and the potential for low back ache. Bending backward counteracts this. It stretches the muscles in the front of your body and lets the muscles in the back shorten, relax, and comfortably reposition themselves.

A gentle back bend will counteract a lot of bad posture and preserve the alignment of the bones in your spine.

Here's how to do it:

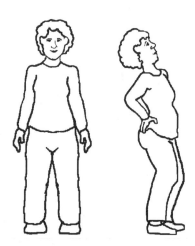

Stand with your feet about as far apart as your shoulders. Place your hands on your buttocks. Let your body slowly arch back as far as is comfortable.

While you relax and breathe gently, imagine the muscles in your lower back letting go. Please, don't force yourself. Use once every hour during the day.

Your goal is a graceful backward arch with your face to the ceiling. If you can't go that far, don't worry. Go only as far as seems safe. It won't take too many repetitions before you can go a little farther. (If you let your jaw relax and go slack while doing this exercise, it will stretch the muscles in the front of your neck.)

If the gentle back bend feels too difficult, you can slowly loosen up and stretch backward by lying on a small cushion placed under the middle and upper back. Take deep breaths to open up the front of your chest.

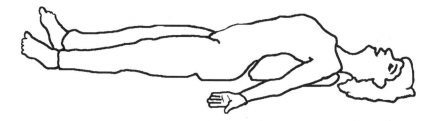

You can also stand close to a wall, lean into it while supporting yourself with your hands, and let your hips swing forward. This will give you a quick, gentle back bend.

TIP: The back bend has an additional benefit. It will make your life easier and more comfortable years from now. Read why on page 126.

Advanced Backward Bending

These exercises will lengthen the front of your body and strengthen your back. Begin them slowly and take your time. Think in terms of weeks and months.

Lie face down on a firm, but comfortable surface. Pillows placed under your lower back and pelvis will keep you from over-arching. If your breasts are sore, you may want to use extra pillows to distribute your weight as comfortably as possible.

When you can lie comfortably in this position, bring your arms into your sides with your elbows bent and your palms down. Look straight ahead and slowly exhale while you gently push your upper body up as far as it will comfortably go.

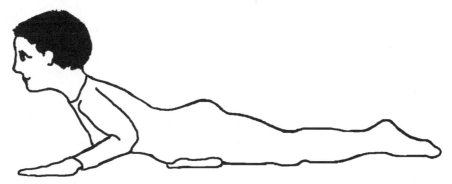

The final step is to push your body all the way up by straightening your arms and pushing upward. As you rise, exhale, and look up at the ceiling. Relax your lower back and buttocks. Let yourself gently down, and rest. Repeat 3 to 5 times.

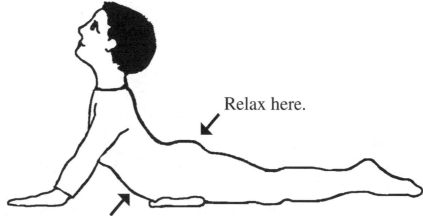

Relax here.

Feel the stretch here.

> **In the last step you put extra weight on your wrists. Doing some wrist extension exercises first (page 132) will help protect them.**

Bending Sideways

Side bends are great for flexibility and for developing the strength needed for all the carrying you'll do as a parent.

Begin any side stretch by reaching and stretching up first, then bending to the side. Forcing your spine to bend without reaching up first can compress and strain the very places you want to liberate.

  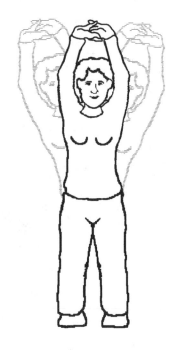

Stand with your legs about shoulder width apart. Reach up high a couple of times alternating hands. Breathe in and out deeply.

Next, clasp your hands over your head and reach up toward the ceiling.

Let your body stay tall while you bend to one side and then come back to the middle. Reach way up each time. Stretch three times on each side.

Keep your head between your arms (not sticking out in front or hanging back) while doing the side bends. This will keep your neck muscles from tightening up. Try to let your jaw relax at the same time. And, even though this seems like a lot to do, tighten the lower belly muscles. Don't hold your breath while you do this stretch (or any other stretch). Exhale each time as you lean to the side.

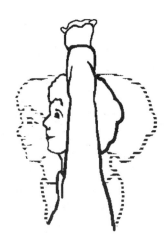

Bending Forward

The "hamstrings" are a series of muscles that overlap and extend from the lower part of your pelvis to below your knees. The upper region, from your buttocks to your knees is usually the tightest. Forward bends stretch this region.

Most people make the mistake of thinking that by bending over to touch their toes, they stretch their hamstrings. The truth is that simple bending over toe touching may not do anything for the hamstrings and can dangerously overstretch the upper back.

The lumbar spine doesn't really bend forward much at all. So what often happens when we try to bend from the waist is that only the upper body bends and it gets strained. Since the hamstrings attach to the base of the pelvis, the real stretch is when the pelvis itself tilts forward.

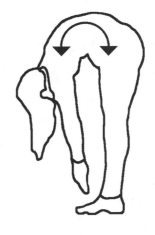

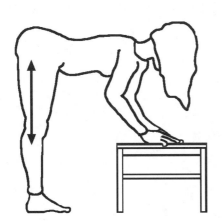

When you do a forward stretch let yourself go forward only as far as you can without bending your lumbar spine at all. Let your hands rest on the edge of a chair, a box, or a pile of books. Adjust the height to accommodate the amount of stretch you can accomplish.

It's good to let the spine relax forward (just don't force it). Let yourself droop forward once in a while after you've mastered the forward bend and know that you are really stretching your hamstrings. One way to do this is to use the same support and slowly lower yourself by bending your arms.

> **TIP: Some people with lower back problems can get muscle spasms from taking a sweater or sweatshirt off over their heads. If this happens to you, try tightening your lower abdominal muscles and making sure that your lower back doesn't flatten out. Keep that lumbar curve.**

The Care and Feeding of the Iliopsoas

Many muscles pass through the lumbar region. The iliopsoas is an important one and it's strongly affected by pregnancy.

One end of this muscle attaches to the front of your upper leg. Then it passes over the edge of your iliac bone and up through the cup of your pelvis to its attachments on the lumbar vertebrae and the upper edge of the iliac bone. The iliopsoas is a powerful muscle and has a role in posture, locomotion, and turning your upper body.

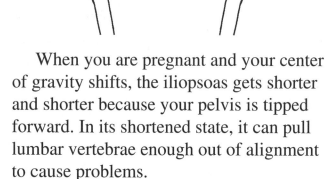

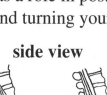

side view

back 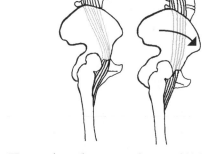 **front**

When you are pregnant and your center of gravity shifts, the iliopsoas gets shorter and shorter because your pelvis is tipped forward. In its shortened state, it can pull lumbar vertebrae enough out of alignment to cause problems.

Two simple stretches will keep your iliopsoas stretched and balanced.

Front Leg Stretch

Stand close to something that will support you if you need it. Tighten your lower abdominal muscles (this will stabilize your pelvis). Raise one leg behind you and grasp the ankle. Pull up gently to achieve the stretch.

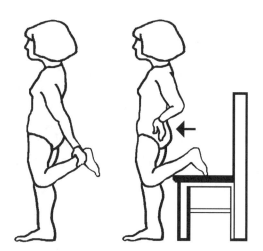

If your pelvis seems unstable, you can modify the stretch by resting your bent leg on a chair behind you and pushing gently forward on the hip.

Bending Backward - Again!

The same back bend stretch that you learned at the beginning of this chapter is great for the iliopsoas as well!

Don't Forget Your Belly

The exercises and stretches in this chapter will limber up your spine and do some strengthening, but the best protection for your lower back is provided by strong abdominal muscles. So, we'll repeat what we said earlier. Make sure you read the chapter on the abdominal muscles and learn the exercises.

Finally...

There are three exercises which are wonderful for all of the muscles that support your lumbar spine. They benefit your sacroiliac, your belly, and just about anything else you can think of in this part of your body.

They are 'The Leg Roll,' 'The Pelvic Tilt,' and 'The Pelvic Clock.' You'll find them in the sacroiliac chapter on pages 76, 77, and 78. If you began reading this book with this chapter, turn back and learn those three now.

Massage

The best possible massage is for you to have your partner take a small, firm rubber ball and work with a gentle rolling pressure along the lower spine on both sides and around the edges of the pelvis just above and below where you can feel bone. You can also do this for yourself, but it's not quite as much fun. When you are getting (or giving) a massage to this area, roll a towel up and slide it under the front crests of your iliac bones or rest your belly and pelvis on a pillow. This will keep your lower back from being strained with too great a curve.

• LIFTING NOTE •

From the standpoint of wear and tear on your body, children were poorly designed. They are too low to the ground! Lifting them up from floor level does more lower back damage than just about anything else.

Infant and toddler equipment contributes to this problem. It's high enough off the ground so that you don't kneel or squat (which would be good for you), and it's so low that you have to stoop over to get your child into or out of it (which is bad for you). Stooping and lifting are a dangerous combination.

Lifting awkwardly is so dangerous and lifting well can make your life so much easier that there are special notes in each of these chapters and two chapters that concentrate mostly on lifting. These are Step by Step (page 34) and Child Equipment (page 27). Read them for more help and practical tips.

No matter how hard you try, the conspiracy of fatigue and soft furniture will always seem to prevent you from sitting erect for very long - particularly when nursing. Sometimes you'll find that you can get stuck in a slump. Even if there are no aches or pains, there may be stiffness and the feeling that you just can't straighten up. You can avoid much of this by standing up carefully.

Here are two things to remember:

- You can use the "basic breath" as a way to get yourself up. Prepare to stand by bringing your baby in close to you. Then, breathe out, suck your lower belly in, pull up on your pelvic floor muscles, and stand. You'll find that you won't have to push yourself up with one hand and, when you suck in rather than push out, you'll avoid extra pressure on your bladder.

- You will be using your abdominals as they should be used, preventing yourself from leaking urine (or at least reducing this), and re-educating your belly muscles so that you reduce back strain.

When you sit for a long time curved over like the letter "C," your spine adjusts itself to this posture. The muscles settle in, the vertebrae shift slightly, and the fluid in your discs changes position. When you stand, you are reversing this curve and you may experience stiffness as the spine resists the change.

If you feel stiff, try this. Put your baby safely down and stand near enough to a wall to be able to reach it with your hands. Push gently into the wall and rock your pelvis backward and forward. You may feel stiffer on one side than the other. In this case, try shifting your weight to one hip and try the backward and forward movement again. Then on the other side. Do more on the side that seems to bring the most relief.

A Last Word

To avoid pain, don't jump straight up from a seated position. Take a moment to prepare yourself while still sitting. Contract your abdominal muscles a couple of times. In short, prepare your body for the move, and then move.

A Look Inside: The Lumbar Spine

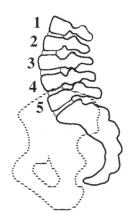

The lumbar spine is made up of five sturdy vertebrae. They run from the bottom of the thoracic spine down to the top of the sacrum.

It has a natural forward curve. Too little curve here is just as bad as too much. Many of us make 'military' posture an ideal. It's not. When the lumbar spine is flattened out it no longer gives your spinal column the resilience and bounce it needs. It also limits the muscles that move your legs and upper body by either tightening them or stretching them too much.

The lumbar spine carries more weight than the rest of your spine and it connects the muscles that control movement above in the thoracic spine and below in the pelvis and legs. It anchors the muscles that raise your legs towards your chest (very important for walking) and those that hold your chest away from your legs (equally important for standing). It does a lot. When it does too much, you know it right away!

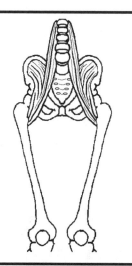	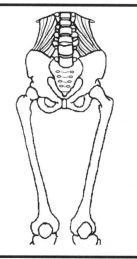	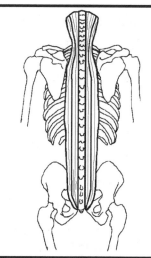
iliopsoas	**quadratus lumborum**	**paraspinals**
It extends the spine, flexes the hip, and directly connects the lower back, pelvis, and legs. This is a vital muscle for walking and for erect posture.	These sheets of muscle attach the ribs, lower spine, and iliac bones. They bend the spine to the sides and keep you from tipping over sideways.	These muscles run the length of your spine. They extend, flex, and rotate your spine, balance the abdominal muscles, and stabilize your posture.

The Hip
(firm those thighs, protect those knees)

COMMON PROBLEMS

Thinking about the hip can be confusing. Sometimes 'the hip' means the actual socket joint where the leg joins the trunk and sometimes it means the whole region to the side of the waist. For most people 'hip pain' is not pain in the actual hip joint, it's pain in the layers of muscle that tie the hip region, lower back, and legs together. Injuries to these muscles can create problems that extend further down the leg to the knee or further up to the lower back or sacroiliac joint.

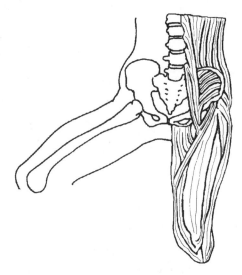

Almost all of the knee problems encountered by new mothers come from muscle imbalances or strains in and around the hip. Most of the muscles that raise, lower, and turn the legs in or out anchor at the hip. Since the knee is a simple back and forth joint most of the turning and twisting movements of the leg come from the hip. If these muscles are chronically tight or are injured, the knee compensates with motions that cause strain, fatigue, and pain.

Women frequently experience some hip soreness late in pregnancy. This is often diagnosed as bursitis, but it's usually caused by pressure on the skin and muscle from your extra weight when you sleep on your side.

Another problem during pregnancy is simple muscle fatigue and soreness from standing. Your center of gravity shifts further and further forward as your baby grows and your pelvis tips forward. This puts a strain on all of the gluteal (buttock) and hip muscles that hold you upright. The resulting discomfort may continue for a while after the birth.

And, yes, firming the thighs is a part of this. All of the muscles that shape the upper legs originate in the hip region. Strengthening and stretching them will have definite therapeutic effects.

Getting Comfortable At Night

If your hips are sore from lying on them, there are some simple things you can do. One is to put a large, solid pillow or bolster behind you. Allow yourself to lean back on it so that your weight rests on a different part of your hip. Another is to alternate the side you sleep on. (Since new mothers don't often get to sleep straight through the night, this will be easy). Or you can get a piece of foam to place under your hip.

Massage

Lie on your stomach with a pillow under your hips. Have your partner massage the sides of the buttocks, particularly the depression in the middle. You can be massaged quite deeply here with good benefits. Self massage for the hip area is easy.

Lie on your back and stroke your lower belly out to the sides and along the pubic bones. You can also reach the muscles at the back of your upper thighs.

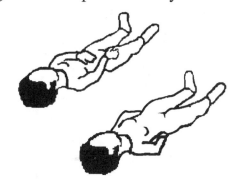

Make two fists and slide them under your buttocks. Roll and rub over them.

Exercises and Stretches

Most of the muscles that move the legs back and forth and sideways begin in the hip region. These motions are controlled by the extensors and flexors of the legs. The most important extensors bringing the leg backward are the gluteus maximus (the big muscle of the buttocks) and the hamstrings that run down the backs of the legs. The principle flexors bringing the leg forward are the iliopsoas (if you've read the lumbar chapter, you've come across this muscle already) and the quadriceps.

About The Quadriceps

front

The quadriceps is actually a set of four muscles. These muscles work together to straighten your knee and bring your leg forward. They begin along the front of the iliac bone and upper thigh, run down the side of the leg, and merge in a tendon that surrounds and attaches to the kneecap before securing everything at the front of the lower leg. Many knee problems are the result of weakness or tightness in the quadriceps. Keeping the quadriceps strong and flexible will protect your knees from injury.

Stretching the Quadriceps

Stand on one leg using something to support your balance. Bring one leg up behind you until you can catch your ankle (if you can't reach it, use a belt to catch your leg). Tighten your lower abdominal muscles by pulling them in, and gently stretch your quadriceps by bringing your ankle toward your buttocks. Bend your leg up straight behind you rather than out to the side. Keep your knee pointed down at the floor. Stretch twice on each side by holding for fifteen to thirty seconds.

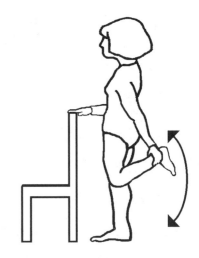

Flat Out Quadriceps Stretch

This is an excellent stretch, but intense. Use it only if you are already quite limber and have no lower back problems.

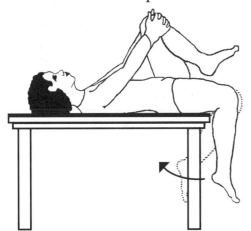

Lie down on a table (or your bed, if it's high enough to let your legs dangle) with your knees just over the edge and your lower legs hanging down. Draw one leg up toward your chest without forcing it too far and hold it. This stabilizes your pelvis.

Swing the dangling leg back under you. This stretches the quadriceps and the iliopsoas muscles.

If you swing your ankle from side to side it will stretch the sides of your thigh. Tighten your lower abdominals as you stretch.

Strengthening the Quadriceps

Sit in a chair and extend first one and then the other leg out straight in front. Make sure you are sitting up straight, but keep the curve in your lower back. Repeat five times for each leg. (If your hamstring muscles are tight, you will feel a pull under your knee.) As your lower leg rises, you'll feel your lower back want to flatten out. Tightening your abdominals and using a pillow at your lower back will keep the curve.

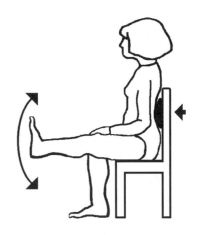

The Wall Slide

This is a more difficult exercise. If you try it and feel any strain, don't use it.

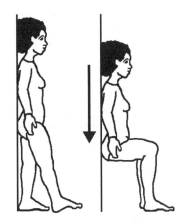

Stand flat against a smooth wall (or the front of your refrigerator). Slide one foot out until it's just beyond the tip of the other foot. Then bring the second foot out the same distance. Bend your knees and slide your back down the wall until your thighs are parallel to the floor. Then push yourself back up. Repeat four times.

Hamstrings

The hamstrings are actually a pair of muscles that attach at the base of your pelvis and run down the back sides of both your legs. The best stretch for them is a standing forward bend which is described in the lumbar chapter on page 93.

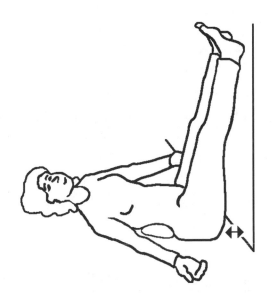

Here is a simpler, passive stretch for those same muscles. Lie on the floor on your back a little way out from the wall. You can adjust the distance depending on how loose your hamstrings are.

Place a towel or very small pillow under the curve of your lower back. Put your feet together up on the wall with your legs straight. Wiggle in closer to the wall until you can feel the stretch and then rest there. Push lightly into the walls with your heels, relax, and then see if you can wiggle even closer.

You can fine tune this stretch by changing the positions of your feet. Tip your toes back toward your body to increase the stretch at the back. Roll out to the side to stretch the insides of the legs, and roll in to stretch the outsides.

> **TIP: The hip muscles are in almost constant use and usually need more stretching than strengthening. You'll find more suggestions on how to stretch safely and effectively on page 53.**

Iliopsoas

The iliopsoas are a pair of muscles that connect the whole middle section of your body. Each is shaped like the letter Y. One upper branch attaches along your lumbar spine and the other branch along the inside of the iliac. They join and run over the front of the pubic bone and down to the inside of the upper leg. The iliopsoas brings your leg forward as you walk and supports you in the standing position.

Iliopsoas Stretches and Exercises

This is the double coupon exercise section. Both of quadriceps stretches are also excellent stretches for the iliopsoas. Another stretch that will do wonders for keeping this important muscle healthy and happy is the simple backbend described in the lumbar chapter on page 90.

Abductors and Adductors

These muscles swing your legs out and in sideways. They stabilize you as you walk. They do this by steadying the leg that carries your weight while the other leg swings forward. This protects the hip joint and pelvis on the weight bearing side.

Stretching Both

Stand with legs comfortably apart. Place your hands on your hips and lean to one side. Keep your legs straight and tighten your lower abdominal muscles while you do this. Hold for several seconds. Then straighten up and relax before leaning to the opposite side.

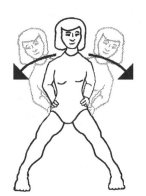

Strengthening the Abductors

Stand with the feet under hips and pointing straight ahead while your arms rest at your sides. Tighten your lower belly muscles. Lift one leg as high as comfortable to the side. At the same time raise the arm on the opposite side. Try holding them up for thirty seconds. Bring them down and do the same for the other arm and leg. Repeat three or more times.

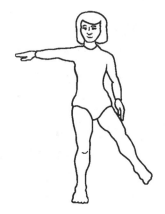

Two Stretches for the Abductors

The Towel Lift

Lie on the side you wish to stretch with your legs out straight. Slide a rolled towel under your thigh about half way between knee and hip. Push up with your arms to get the stretch. This will also stretch a major muscle that lies between the bottom of the ribs and the back portion of your pelvis, the quadratus lumborum.

Crossover Side Bend

Stand with your feet as far apart as your hips. Place one foot in front of the other and bend away from the side you wish to stretch. Try this stretch first with your hands on your hips. If it's easy for you, raise the opposite arm over your head (this can also help with painful menstrual crampsa). You can also try this stretch with one foot behind. Try it both ways and see which is better for you

Stretching the Adductors

Sit on the floor with your legs straight and spread apart as far as possible. Sitting comfortably in this position may mean sitting on a cushion or folded blanket.

Feel for the curve in your lower back. If it has flattened out, raise yourself until you can feel it. Then, lean forward until you can feel the stretch. Hold it for a while. Come back up, slide your legs a little further apart, and lean forward again.

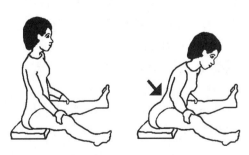

Check each time to make sure that you keep the curve in your lower back.

A Gentler Stretch

If the last stretch strains you or you have difficulty keeping the curve in your lower back, use this to loosen yourself up.

Lie on your back and draw your knees up to the level of your waist. Place your hands so that you are reaching between your legs and your hands are cupped around the knees. Let your legs sprawl out to the sides until you can feel the stretch. Hold for fifteen or twenty seconds and then bring your legs back to the center. Lower your feet to the floor one at a time. Repeat several times.

Strengthening the Adductors

Foot Roll and Clench

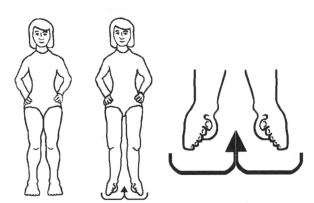

Stand with your feet close together. Tighten your pelvic floor, buttocks, and lower abdominals by pulling them all in and then roll your feet to the outer edges so that you're standing on the sides. Hold for several seconds and then relax down onto your feet. Repeat three or four times.

Ball Squeeze

Lie on your back with your arms out to your sides. Bring your knees up with your feet on the floor and keep the curve in your lower back. Place a large ball or a very firm cushion between your knees and squeeze against it. Hold the squeeze for a count of five and then relax. Repeat several times.

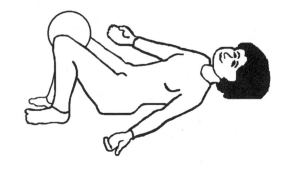

• WALKING NOTE •

As you walk along, notice how your feet fall on the ground. On a rainy or snowy day or walking in soft soil or at the beach, you can look at the foot prints you leave. Do you toe out or toe in? Do both feet point the same way, or do they point in different directions? Two of your abductor muscles, the gluteus medius and the tensor fascia lata, help to rotate the leg and foot to the inside or the outside.

Extremes or an unevenness in toeing in or toeing out can indicate muscle imbalances in the rotators. Over the years, one becomes too tight and the other becomes over stretched. Such imbalances can cause hip and knee pain. If this seems to be your case, consult with a health care practitioner. Exercises can help correct this, although in some cases you may need deep massage to free up the muscles, shoe inserts, or special shoes to correct the problem.

A Last Word

Everything in your body, particularly every muscular thing, is interconnected. The abdominal muscles (which support your back) and the pelvic floor muscles (which support your insides), interweave with the same muscles that support and surround your hips. Read the chapters on the pelvic floor (page 13) and the on the abdominals (page 61) to find out how to strengthen these muscles as well.

A Look Inside: The Hip

Your legs are moved by the muscles of the hip and trunk. Extensors and flexors move them from back and forth. Abductors and adductors move them from side to side and stabilize your stride as you move. The rotators turn your legs in and out.

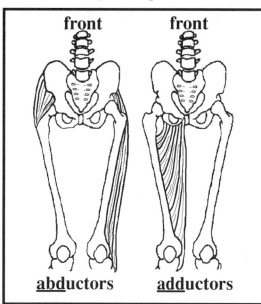

front   front

abductors   adductors

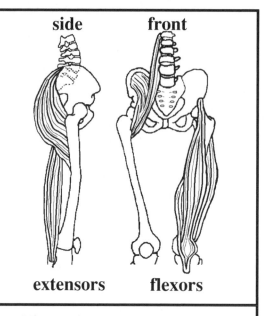

side   front

extensors   flexors

The abductors are the gluteus medius and the tensor fascia lata. They connect the upper rim of the iliac bone with the leg along the outer side as far down as the knee.

The adductors are a long, triangular wedge of muscles that attach to the lower edge of the pubic bone and along the inside of the upper leg.

The major extensors of the hip are the hamstrings and the gluteus maximus (the big muscles that gives shape to the buttocks). The major flexors are the iliopsoas and the quadriceps.

All of these muscles play an important role in walking and in supporting your upright posture.

The tensor fascia lata and the gluteus medius also act as rotators. The tensor fascia lata turns the leg in and the gluteus medius turns it out. They work with another set of muscles, the deep lateral rotators, which lie buried deep in the center of your buttocks.

Don't worry about the names of all these muscles. The important thing is that they strongly tie your body together. When they are healthy and strong they support and protect everything from your lower back and sacroiliac joints down to your knees.

The Cervical Spine

(it can be a pain in the neck)

COMMON PROBLEMS

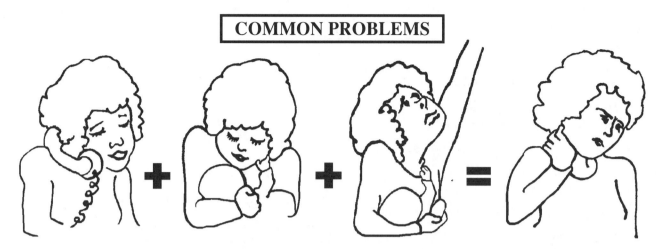

Your neck works all the time. It also gets a lot of abuse. Long phone calls with the receiver caught between your shoulder and chin, nursing in one position, or working with your head bent forward, all strain the muscles of the neck. When you hold your head in awkward positions for a long time, you shorten and cramp the muscles on one side and overstretch those on the other.

Pregnancy adds other strains. Your ribs are pushed up to make room for your growing baby. This changes the length of the neck muscles that attach to the top ribs and they work harder. The muscles that run down the sides of your neck (the scalenes) are often affected. Important blood vessels and nerves pass in between these muscles on the way to the arms, hands, and chest. When the muscles cramp, they can constrict the blood vessels and nerves that pass through them. This is one of the reasons why pregnant women sometimes experience trouble with numbness and tingling in the arms and hands.

Some of these symptoms fade away naturally after the birth, but you will still be vulnerable to headaches, stiffness, and aching. Over long periods, tense muscles can create enough pull on the bones of the neck to force them slightly out of position. This causes pain, clicking or popping sounds, and limitations in your ability to move freely. The major symptom of neck trouble is the stiff neck, although warnings may come from your arms, hands, lower back, and, surprisingly, from headaches.

> **PAIN ALERT: Many people with lower back problems develop neck pain. Your body automatically compensates for any injury - often by changing your posture. The new posture can strain other parts of your body by forcing them to take over some of the work of balancing.**

A Pain in the Neck (or head or arm)

Some headaches come from the misalignment of the bones of the neck. Tight, cramped muscles can pull a vertebra slightly out of place. The bone may then press on the nerves or blood supply for a specific region of your head.

Each of the numbered areas on the head, neck, and arms can be affected by misalignments of the corresponding cervical vertebrae (they are numbered 1-7 from the skull down).

The nerves for each of these regions leave the spinal column at the level of the cervical vertebrae with which they are labled. If you carry or lift on one side more than the other or habitually tip your head in just one direction, the muscles on that side will be tighter and the muscles on the other side weaker. Such imbalances can pull the vertebrae out of place and cause stiffness, headache, nausea, dizziness, or strange sensations down the arms.

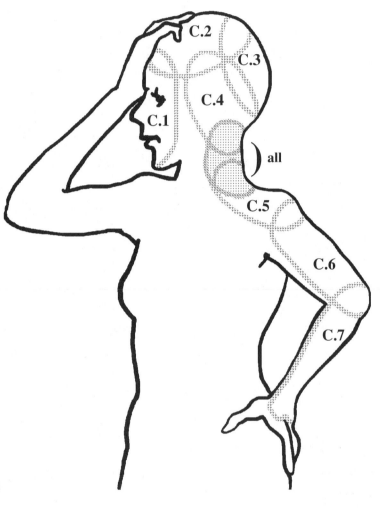

Some misalignments occur slowly as tense muscles pull on the bones and some are the result of sudden movements or a blow.

The muscles of the neck attach to the cervical vertebrae and to the skull, shoulders, and back. Each individual vertebra is an attachment point for many different muscles! You can see why what happens in one place affects many others.

TIP: Numb fingers can also be caused by wrist or thoracic problems. If this happens to you read the chapters on the wrist (page 129) and the thoracic spine (page 117) for other possible causes.

Massage

A Gentle Rub

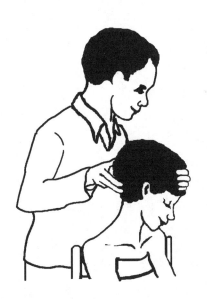

At the base of your skull at the back of your head there is a ridge of bone that runs from ear to ear. This is called the nuchal line. Have your partner or a friend gently rub the nuchal line. Many of the neck and shoulder muscles attach here as well as the muscles that run up the length of your back, so it's a very dynamic place. (You can do this massage yourself, but it's not as easy and not as relaxing.)

A Self Massage

This is a light massage for neck relaxation.

- Gently stroke from behind your ear down and forward to the base of your neck where your collar bones meet. This is the sternal notch. Let your finger tips rest here for a moment.

- Stroke along your collar bones from the shoulders into the center.

- Rub softly along the lower edge of the collar bones, working from the sternal notch to the shoulder. Push upward gently as you go.

- Lightly squeeze and rub the blades of muscle that slope up from your shoulders to the base of your neck.

Stretching

Sit up straight in a chair. Clasp hands with your thumbs down behind your head and your fingers interlaced under the base of the skull. Squeeze, relax, and then gently lift up the back of your head for 3 to 5 seconds. Relax while breathing out and let your shoulders droop. Turn your head to the sides to see if it moves more freely.

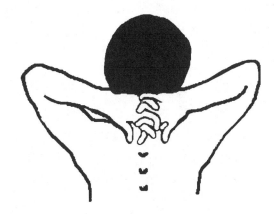

Exercises

An Essential Exercise

If you only have time to do one neck exercise, this is it. It's simple, easy to do, and it will immediately relax you.

There's a little notch at the center top of your rib cage, just at the meeting of your two collar bones. This is called the sternal notch. Let your hand rest lightly on your chest with the tip of your index finger on the notch. Relax, then slowly breathe up and into your hand. Imagine your breath lifting your hand. Let your shoulders relax downward as your hand lifts. Do this several times in a row every hour for a day or two and see if it makes a difference.

This straightens you from the mid-back on up. It brings all of the vertebrae in your neck back into a strong supporting column under your head.

The next four exercises will help your neck be relaxed and strong. In the best of all possible worlds, you'd do each exercise, six repetitions, six times a day. If you have a tendency to develop neck problems, make it a priority. Otherwise, do the best you can. Everything you do for yourself helps. All of these exercises will be most effective if you sit on the front edge of a straight chair.

The Relaxed Shrug

Sit comfortably. Let your arms hang loosely at your sides. Position your head so that your ear lobes are on a line down through your shoulders and hips. Raise your shoulders slightly and then let them drop away from your ears. Do this six times.

As you do this, be aware of how the muscles in your neck connect with your shoulder blades, collar bones, and down your spine. You can expand this exercise by making imaginary circles with your shoulders, rolling them up and back and around and then reversing it.

> **CAUTION NOTE: The neck is a delicate region. Do these exercises gently. If your symptoms are related to a blow or make it difficult to move, don't exercise or stretch the neck. Seek medical attention. You will probably be asked to rest and possibly to wear a supporting collar until the muscles and ligaments heal.**

The Turtle

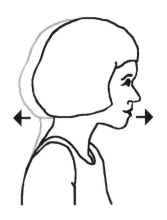

Move your head backward and forward, slowly. Bring your head back so that your ear lines up with your shoulders. You don't have to go too far. (If it's hard to swallow, that's too much.) Then move it forward (again, not too far) along a straight line. The distance back and forth can be as little as an inch and a half. To avoid tipping your head up and down, look at something straight ahead of you.

The Neck Roll

Neck rolls can be deliciously relaxing. You can keep them that way by not forcing your neck to go back too far. "Lolling" might be a better word than rolling. Go only as far to each side as is comfortable, and don't try to make it all the way around - that's for owls.

Your goal is to make the rolls equally comfortable in all directions. If you feel at all tight, try doing the sternal notch exercise (The Essential Exercise on the previous page) before you begin. Holding on to the sides of your chair will give you a greater stretch.

Rowing

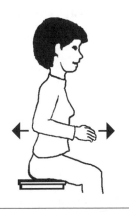

Line up your ears with your shoulders and hips. Bend your elbows so that your hands are parallel to the floor about midway between hip and neck. Use your shoulder blades to row your arms back and forth. Remember to line up ears, shoulders, and hips. If your head is thrust forward, it defeats the point of this exercise.

TIP (for working parents): If your job keeps you sitting for long periods with your head in one position, do these exercises as often as possible. If you use a computer, make sure the monitor is adjusted so that your neck is at a comfortable angle. You should be able to read center screen with your head lined up over your hips and shoulders. You should be able to scan from top to bottom without having to move your neck.

Two Restful Exercises

If you wore yourself out with the earlier exercises, here are two that will do an amazing amount of good and you can do them lying down.

The first is for late evenings, your child's nap time, or when a partner is around to cover for you.

Roll up a towel so that it's about three inches thick. Lie on it so that it runs down the length of your spine, but not under your head. Your arms should rest out to the sides with your hands palm up. As you lie over the towel, your chest will open up and your shoulders drop back onto the floor. This counteracts the hunched over posture we all get into. Remember to take deep relaxing breaths. Do this for five minutes or longer.

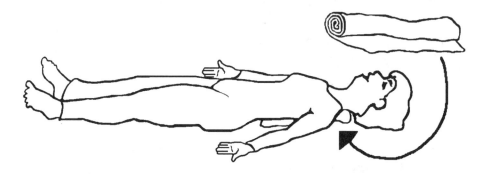

The next one is a little more active. You can do it when you wake up in the morning or just before going to bed at night. Lie on your back. Raise your arms up over your chest and clasp your hands together. Rock your arms slowly from side to side. Let your head roll in either the same direction as your arms or in the opposite direction, whichever seems more comfortable.

Do this for five minutes or so. You can try moving your clasped hands to different positions above your face and body. Different positions will relax and stretch different parts of your upper back.

• A SLEEP NOTE •

You spend about a third of each twenty-four hours sleeping (or trying to anyway). Spending the night with your neck in an awkward position is almost guaranteed to result in stiffness or headaches the next day. You deserve a good night's rest.

Not so good!   **Great!**

If you sleep on your side, make sure your pillow supports your head so that your neck isn't tipped too far up or down. Alternate sides when you can.

Ahhhh...

If you sleep on your back, tuck a towel under your neck to support the curve of your cervical spine, or sleep with a special pillow that does this for you.

Beware!

Try not to sleep on your stomach! This is a habit that you can (and should) break. Have you ever noticed that when you sleep on your stomach you sometimes wake with numb arms or hands or feeling very groggy?

When you sleep on your stomach, your neck bends and turns in such a way that as much as 30% of the blood supply to your head and arms can be cut off. Worse, as you get older this percentage will increase. The symptoms of numbness, tingling, and hypoxia (the grogginess) when you wake are usually the result of this decreased circulation. Sleep on your side or back and with your neck protected and comfortable.

> **TIP: Don't nap in awkward positions. Arrange yourself so that your neck is comfortably supported. Lie down to nap whenever possible.**

• LIFTING NOTE •

People who are prone to stiff necks and upper back soreness need to be careful about doing things above their heads. Lifting the baby up high while arching back is a classic parent posture. It's been immortalized in countless commercials. Unfortunately, it can cause neck and upper shoulder problems.

You can safely lift your child above your head with a little preparation. Bring the baby up close to your body, elbows bent and give her a hug. While you hug, bring your shoulder blades together and relax them a couple of times. Then lift. Lift evenly with both arms and don't force your head too far back.

Carrying your child on your shoulders with legs straddling your neck can bring on headaches and a stiff neck. If you or your partner like to carry your child this way, do it for short periods. Problems most often occur when you find yourself at a fair, rally, or parade and carry your child like this for too long a time.

After, do a few neck stretches to loosen up. This isn't a chapter about hips, but if you always carry your child on one hip, pay attention to what also happens to your neck. You'll see why alternating sides is a good idea.

Alternating sides for any kind of carrying will benefit your cervical spine (and the rest of you as well). Stiff necks often start with the tense, overworked muscles across the upper back and chest that come from too much strain on one side of the body. If you regularly carry a shoulder bag, remind yourself to change sides occasionally.

CAUTION: If you have a stiff neck or upper back tension, be extra careful when you reach for something over your head. If it's heavy, use both arms and shrug your shoulders before lifting. Or make yourself higher by using a stool or chair. Always reaching with the same arm can create a muscle imbalance, so alternate sides as often as you can.

Most women spend feeding time adoring their babies. You're probably the same. Of course, while you do this your neck is bent forward for a long time and it's easy to forget to move.

If you bottle feed or have a baby that prefers one breast over the other, it's even easier to forget. Unfortunately, too much time in the same position can lead to a stiff neck, headaches, or just an overall cranky, pent-up feeling.

To prevent this, follow these suggestions:

- Alternate sides regularly.

- Remind yourself to look around once in a while.

- Use the neck exercises in this book whenever possible.

A Last Word

Your changing table isn't a place where you encounter a lot of neck strain. It is a good place to take a moment to relax your neck and move your head around. Try this during a couple of changings each day:

Place your hand on your sternal notch and inhale as if to lift the hand up. This will straighten out your head and shoulders and ease you right down to your mid-back. Relax and exhale slowly. If your baby still seems content, do the "turtle" exercise (page 111) and a neck roll or two.

TIP: Your changing table gets a lot of use. Make sure that it's a height that you find comfortable. The chapter on the changing table (page 23) has some ideas and suggestions.

A Look Inside: The Cervical Spine

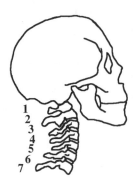

A lot is packed into your neck. The seven cervical vertebrae are surrounded by the muscles, ligaments, and nerves that make the movement of the head and neck possible. The veins and arteries of the neck carry the blood that nourish your head and brain. The nerves that supply your arms and upper body leave the spinal column at the level of the neck. It is also the location of the sensors that help you balance.

The top two vertebrae have a unique shape. They are called the atlas and the axis. These two fit one on top of the other under the skull. They pivot and turn so that the head can rotate as well as tip back and forth. The lower five move back and forth and from side to side easily, but turn only slightly.

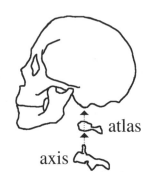

The neck is crowded with the muscle groups that move and stabilize your head, neck, and shoulders. They connect the cervical vertebrae to your shoulder blades, collar bones, skull and rib cage.

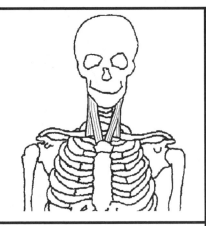

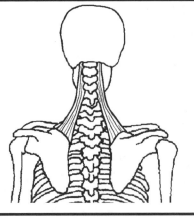

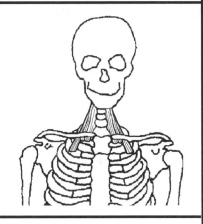

sternoclidomastoids	**levator scapulae**	**scalenes**
This pair attaches at the skull just behind the jaw and runs down to the sternum and collar bone. They tilt your head up and back and they also turn it from side to side.	When the shoulder blades are fixed in one place by other muscles, they pull your head back. When your head is held steady, they raise the shoulder blades.	The scalenes lie on each side of your neck and attach the vertebrae to the ribs. They tip the head from side to side and, when they act together, pull your neck forward.

The Thoracic Spine
(For Every Back, A Front)

COMMON PROBLEMS

All of us hunch over. When we work, care for children, drive, or read, we bend forward in concentration. And while one part of the body hunches in concentration, the rest slumps. This combination of half-concentrating and half-slumping isn't good. Muscles begin to twitch, twinge, and ache. This is particularly true for the upper back, the thoracic spine.

As shoulders pull forward, the muscles between the shoulder blades stretch. When they are chronically stretched, they weaken. As they weaken, they become more vulnerable to strains and pains and they force other muscles to work harder. The muscles on the front of the chest shorten more. This pulls your shoulders even farther forward. There is a vicious circle at work, and it's working against you.

Upper back muscle tension can cause a lot more trouble than just soreness. Your collar bones and shoulder blades together form a yoke of bones that sits around the top of your rib cage. This yoke is the platform and attachment place for the muscles that move and support your head, neck, and arms. Problems here, either with muscles or joints, can echo in lots of other places.

Thoracic Outlet Syndrome is one of the conditions that can often be triggered by the body changes of pregnancy and then continue on through the early post-partum period. It is troublesome, but easily treatable in all but its most chronic form.

> **TIP: It can be hard to read a book like this which lists problem after problem. Don't let yourself get bogged down with worrying about conditions that don't affect you. Do take good care of yourself.**

Thoracic Outlet Syndrome

In addition to ordinary aches and pains, you may notice numbness and weakness in your hands and arms. You may wake after about an hour's sleep with arm tingling and pain. If so, it's possible you have Thoracic Outlet Syndrome. This may sound like a plumbing problem, but its got more to do with your collarbone and neck muscles than your colon.

The Thoracic Outlet

The "thoracic outlet" is the space between your collarbone (clavicle) and the top or first rib. The nerves and arteries that supply your arms and hands leave the spinal column at the neck and pass through the thoracic outlet.

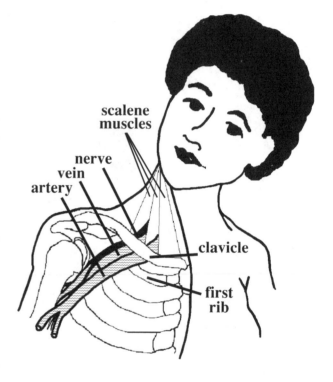

This condition often occurs in pregnancy because the ribs move up to accommodate the growing baby by as much as one to two inches. This pushes the top ribs much closer to the collar bones. During pregnancy and in the early post-partum period, your muscles are also swollen with extra fluid. The smaller rib space and the swelling combine to constrict both the nerves and the arteries of your arms and hands.

When nerves and arteries are pinched or restricted, you will often have symptoms in the parts of your body that they serve. In this case, it's your arms and hands.

Gravity and daily chores hunch us over, pulling our collarbones forward and down. Some women experience numbness and weakness in the hands and arms during the day. For others, only the change of position and deeper relaxation of sleep allow this space to open up again. Restored circulation causes a "pins and needles" sensation and sometimes enough pain to wake you after falling asleep. This condition isn't only one of pregnancy. The physical work of parenting can be enough to create the problem.

> **TIP: Hand tingling and numbness can also be symptoms of wrist or neck problems. Check these chapters as well (wrist on page 129 and neck on page 107). With any serious condition, consult your doctor.**

WHAT TO DO ABOUT IT

Stretching and exercising the muscles that attach to the shoulders, shoulder blades, and collarbones will help keep you free from injury and pain, and leave you feeling much more energetic.

Self Massage

You can help the thoracic exercises along by gently massaging the muscles before you begin. Another good time to massage these muscles is during a warm shower.

The pectorals (of body building fame) are the strong muscles that run from the upper chest to the shoulder. When the shoulders are constantly tense and pulled forward, the pectorals become chronically shortened and tense. To massage them, place your four fingers in your arm pit with your thumb up and fitted into the small cup-like depression where your collarbone, shoulder, and chest come together. Gently knead the muscles there. As you knead, work from the shoulder to the center of your chest and back again.

The slope of muscle that rises from your shoulders to your neck is the upper edge of a busy set of muscles called the trapezius. They lift your shoulder blades, turn your neck, and tilt your head. You can relieve some of the tension that builds up in them by gently rubbing in small circles along the surface and by squeezing it gently between thumb and forefinger.

The sternoclidomastoid muscles tilt your head and turn it to the side. If you walk around, as many of us do, with your head lowered and your chin stuck out, these muscles become chronically shortened and tight. A gentle stroking from the base of the skull to your collarbone will feel good. It will also help loosen you up for any of the neck stretches.

TIP: We all slump. We feel that slumping is relaxing. Take the time to retrain yourself. Make slumping an effort. A relaxed and open chest is much more restful and a lot less painful.

Exercises and Stretches

Opening the Chest

Exercise can help you get your upper back under control and either prevent Thoracic Outlet Syndrome or relieve the symptoms. Below is a three part exercise that you can begin slowly and then extend as your shoulder region becomes looser. You can do it in bed or on the floor. Lie on a comfortable rug or a doubled over blanket.

Relax on your back with your knees up and your arms slightly out from your sides, palms up. Do this for five minutes in the morning and five minutes in the evening. (Really relax and try not to think about anything that needs to be done.)

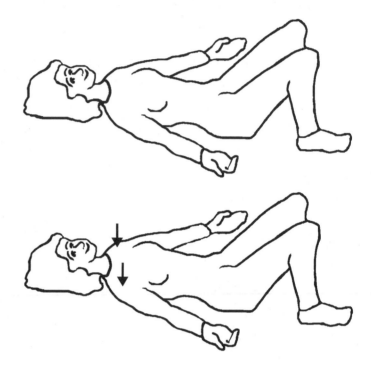

Gently push your shoulders back into whatever soft surface you are on. Let your lower back stay relaxed, not flat to the floor and not arched up too high. Hold for a count of five. Then rest. Repeat this five times and then relax completely.

Bring your hands (palms still up) over your head and down above your so that your palms are on the floor. If your arms don't go that far, try putting a pillow or two above your head so that your arms can go as far as comfortable. Rest there for awhile. Remember, the goal is relaxation and stretching, not punishment.

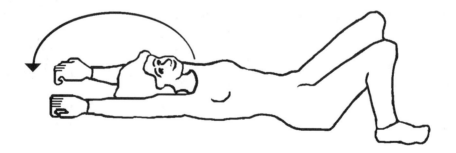

> **TIP: Breathe in, and as you breathe out, tighten your lower belly muscles while you lift your arms. This will help keep your lower back from arching up too far from the floor.**

Some Quickies

These are a couple of stretches and toners that you can use after any period of forward concentration such as nursing or driving. All of them can be done sitting down. Each takes less than a minute, so don't neglect them (or yourself)!

Sit comfortably. Clasp your hands behind your head at the base of the skull. If this is hard, just let your fingertips meet. Bring your elbows back as far as you can without straining. Let them relax forward, then bring them back again. Repeat four times. Keep your chin in, if it sticks out in front, you won't be getting the stretch. This is particularly good for relieving tight cramps between the shoulder blades.

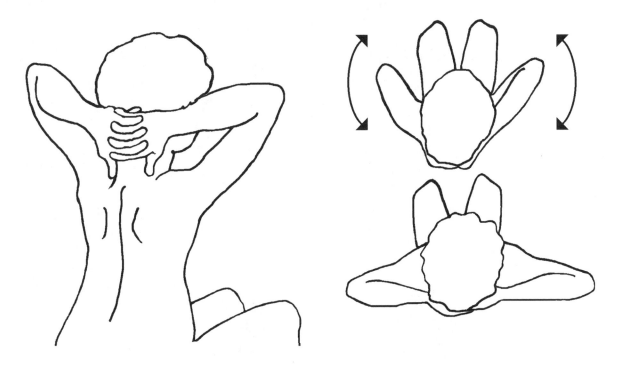

Hold your hands up to the sides, level with your head. Alternate reaching above your head with each hand.

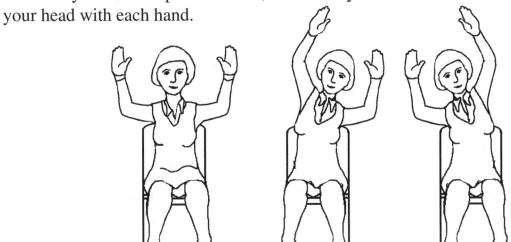

More Quickies

Cross your arms in front of you and rest your hands on your thighs. Pull your shoulders blades together behind your back. As they come together, allow them to pull your arms up and out to either side and inhale deeply. If it is comfortable, you can hold light weights in your hands while you do it.

Lay your hands on your thighs, palms down. Relax your shoulder blades . Turn your palms up. Feel how this opens up your chest. Now bring your shoulder blades together. Use this movement to slide your hands back along your thighs. Then reverse it. Repeat several times.

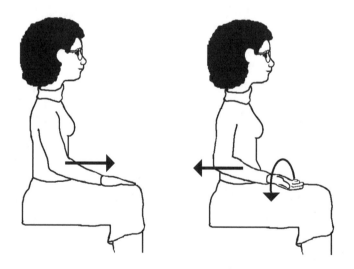

TIP FOR WORKING MOTHERS: If you work at a keyboard, these exercises will save you a lot of mid-back discomfort. They only take moments and can be done at your seat. Do them frequently, if you can. They also relieve some neck strain. (I used the first one on the previous page about every fifteen minutes while typing this and it helped.)

Pectoral Assistance

Strengthening the muscles that pull your shoulder blades together will balance the overuse and tightening of the pectorals. There are two good exercises for this.

You'll need a strip of something elastic about four feet long. You can use a length of sewing elastic ½ inch wide or wider, a lot of thick rubber bands looped together, or you can buy a commercial product call a "Theraband™." (We tried several brands of panty hose, but they didn't have enough stretch.)

Lie on your back on a comfortable surface. Your legs can be flat or you can raise your knees, whichever you prefer. You could do this standing up, but most people stick their chins out when they do and that counteracts some of the benefits. Lying down keeps your head in the best position.

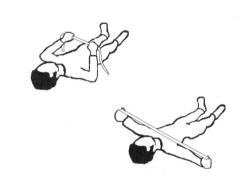

With your elbows on the floor, grasp the stretching strip above your chest. Slowly and steadily straighten your arms out to the sides and bring your shoulder blades together. Tighten your belly muscles as you move your arms. Hold, then let them relax back to the beginning position above your chest.

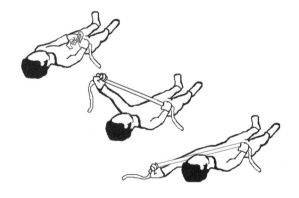

Take an end of your strip in each hand and place both hands on one hip. Slowly and steadily raise the arm from the opposite side of your body (if your hands are on your right hip, raise the left arm). Keep your arm straight. Bring it up and over your head and down to the floor behind you. Let it be pulled back to your hip. Now do the same on the other side.

Do both exercises four times each or more, but don't over do! If you feel a strain, stop. If you get bored, try alternating the side stretches with the crossover stretches.

> **TIP: These will also help your abdominals, but only if you exhale and pull your lower belly muscles in while you do the exercises.**

The Armchair Exercise (ahhhh...)

This is a good antidote for Thoracic Outlet problems, particularly if you find yourself waking up after about an hour of sleep with a painful pins and needles sensation in your arms or hands.

The good part of this "exercise" is that it's completely passive. The bad part is that it doesn't eliminate the sensation. When you fall asleep the change of position and relaxation takes the pressure off the thoracic outlet. As circulation is restored, you feel the pins and needles and this is what wakes you up. By using the armchair exercise you take the pressure off and feel the pins and needles before you go to sleep.

Here's how to do it.

Sit in a chair with arm rests. You are going to sit for a while with your arms pushing your shoulder yoke upwards. If your chair's arm rests aren't high enough, put pillows on them or take the seat cushion out. Experiment to find which is best for you. Relax and make sure you are letting the chair arms do the lifting. Let your neck and shoulders relax. It may take five to ten minutes until you experience the sensation.

Stay relaxed in your chair until the feeling of pins and needles goes away. Later you should have a good night's sleep (well, let's be realistic about the life of a new mother and say a better night's sleep).

TIP: Beware of your television set! When you're tired and flop in front of it, strange things can happen. Strong beams will pull you into a slump and your shoulders will roll forward. Resist these beams by changing positions often, sitting well, and by bringing your shoulders back at regular intervals. Use pillows to support your lower back.

Seize the Moment

Stretches can be done anywhere and anytime - and should be! Use your whole environment to help you. You'll discover that you can grab a short and helpful stretch while in the middle of just about anything.

You can use the top of the refrigerator or the edge of an open cabinet for this one. Grab an edge slightly higher than your head. Your hands should be about as far apart as your shoulders. Keep your knees slightly bent and let your upper body relax downward.

Or, reach up and grab the upper edge of a door frame. Stand on a book or box, if necessary. Let your body hang down, but with your feet still supporting most of your weight.

Up Against the Wall (for those desperate moments...)

Stand with your back against a wall. Let your heels, calves, buttocks, upper back, and head touch the surface.

Bring your arms up to your sides, elbows bent and touching the wall, and hands at about the level of your head. Breathe in.

Breathe out and as you exhale, slide your hands up and out. Pull your lower belly in while you exhale. This will keep your back from arching too far out. Only go as far as is comfortable and keep your elbows touching the wall. Hold for thirty seconds to a minute. Relax and slide your arms back down. Do four times.

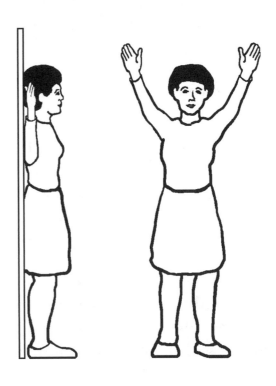

Backbends

This stretch is here and in the chapter on the lumbar spine because it is so important. It's important for you now and even more important for you in later life. A three year study conducted by a researcher named Sinaki checked the effects of different exercises on post-menopausal woman who had thoracic fractures as a result of osteoporosis. The women were divided into three groups. One group of women did toe touching, one group did backbends, and one group did no special exercises.

After three years the results were compared and they were startling. Eighty percent of the toe touchers and sixty percent of the no exercisers had another fracture of the thoracic spine. Only sixteen percent of the backbend group suffered another fracture. You can see why you need this exercise. After you learn it, teach your mother, your sister, your aunt, and any other women you know.

Follow these steps for a simple and relaxing back bend.

As with any exercise, don't push yourself. Forcing yourself to stretch far beyond what is your present range of motion can cause muscle injury. Be gentle and keep at it.

Stand with your feet about as far apart as your shoulders. Place your hands on your buttocks. Let your body slowly arch back, but only as far as is comfortable. Please, don't force yourself. Do this once every hour during the day. Allow yourself to relax and breathe gently. Imagine the muscles in your lower back relaxing and letting go.

Your goal is a graceful backwards arch with your face looking up to the ceiling. If you can't go this far, don't worry. Go as far as seems reasonable and safe. It won't take too many repetitions before you can do a little more. (If you let your jaw go slack while doing this exercise, it will stretch the muscles in the front of your neck.)

> **TIP: The toe touchers in the study used the 'just bend over and go for it' toe touch. This overstretches and strains the upper back, particularly if you don't stretch in the opposite direction. The forward bend (page 93) will show you how to stretch your hamstrings safely.**

• NURSING NOTE •

Feeding your baby is wonderful. It can also be a source of muscle strain because you will curl forward around your baby every time you nurse or bottle feed and you'll forget everything else.

Use these simple ideas to avoid thoracic aches and pains.

- Make yourself comfortable before you begin.

- Alternate the side you feed on. If you bottle feed, you need to be particularly aware of this. Full or empty breasts are not going to remind you to shift from side to side.

- When you finish, do a few back bending stretches.

• LIFTING NOTE •

Well, ok, in this case we're giving you a reaching note.

Shoulder blades are moving platforms for many of the muscles that control your neck and arms. They slide and pivot across your back. When they can't move freely, your shoulders, arms, and neck are restricted. The rest of your body then has to twist and strain while reaching. Releasing the shoulder blades will add the extra reach without the stress. Try this:

Reach up as high as you can on a wall. Note how high you can comfortably reach.

Now, before reaching again, tighten the muscles that bring your shoulder blades together. Roll your shoulders to bring them back and down. Then relax and let the shoulder blades slide up with your reach. You'll find that you can reach just as high or higher without stretching and straining.

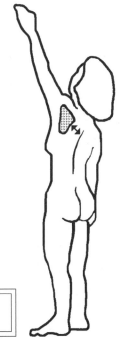

TIP: If it's higher than this, get a stool.

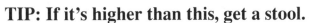

A Look Inside: The Thoracic Spine

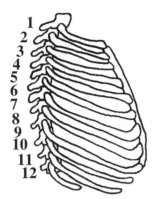

The thoracic spine begins at the base of your neck and runs to the bottom of the ribs. There are twelve thoracic vertebrae. Each one is connected to a pair of ribs. Some of the muscles that attach to this part of your spine run down into the lower back region and up to the base of your skull. Muscle tension here can cause massive headaches

Some of the parts of the nervous system that affect sweating, heart flutter, and nausea are located along the thoracic spine. You may have these symptoms, if this area is strained.

The thoracic yoke rests on top of the rib cage and encircles the neck. It is made up of the collarbones (clavicles), shoulder joints, and shoulder blades.

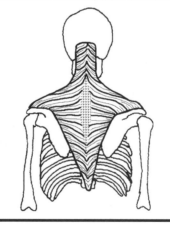

clavicle
shoulder joint
shoulder blade

The bony structrue of the shoulder yoke is only half the story. The other half is the web of muscles that do the actual work. Here are a few.

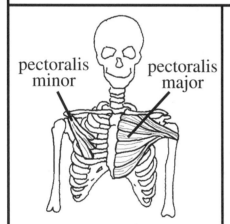

pectoralis minor

pectoralis major

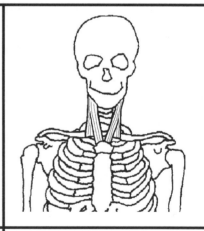

pectorals	trapezius	sternoclidomastoids
Their job is pushing, lifting, and applying pressure to things in front of you. The broad major pectorals lie over the minor ones on each side.	This set of muscles lifts and lowers your shoulders, tilts your head, and helps turn your neck. It connects the base of the skull to the bottom of the thoracic spine.	These muscles attach at the skull just behind the jaw and at the sternum and clavicle. They tilt your head up and turn your head from side to side.

The Hand That Rocks The Cradle
(is attached to a wrist)

COMMON PROBLEMS

Your wrist is a remarkably strong and stable joint considering all the hard work it does. During pregnancy and the early post-partum months, it needs extra care.

Almost one third of all expectant mothers have some wrist pain. The two major causes are swelling and muscular stress. By the end of your pregnancy you may have as much as 40% more fluid in your body and all that liquid creates swelling. The wrist is a narrow space crowded with two large bones, eight small bones, nine tendons, two major nerves and several blood vessels. Everything gets squeezed when swelling occurs. The combination of lifting and swelling can cause nerve compression and pain. It may also force the small bones of the wrist out of place. An aching wrist, numbness, tingling in the hand, and weakness in the fingers are all symptoms of possible wrist problems.

After your baby is born, your wrists remain vulnerable. Some of the extra fluid may stay in your tissues for as long as six months after the birth. You will also be doing a lot more lifting! Some of that lifting requires a kind of scooping and "cradling" gesture. At other times your wrist will be in a position similar to that of holding a hammer. Both put considerable strain on the wrist.

The 'Cradle'

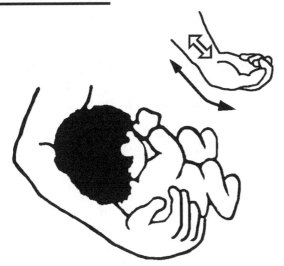

In the "cradle" position the wrist is flexed or curled toward your body.

When it's in this position, the flexor muscles that pull the hand up and in (the fat arrow) are shortened and the extensor muscles that pull the hand backward (the thin arrow) are stretched. Problems arise when this goes on for too long. The flexors become chronically shortened and the extensors become stretched and weak.

The pain from "cradle" strain frequently appears when the wrist is bent in the opposite direction.

The 'Hammer' Grip

Another position that strains the wrist is the "cocked" or hammer grip. This is the same one that causes problems for carpenters.

Carpenters use the grip to raise the hammer for a blow. Parents use it to support a sitting child or when picking up a child by taking her under the arms. If you're both a carpenter and a parent, you're going to have to watch this one! This grip pulls some of the thumb's tendons taut over bone and when it happens too often, a painful tendonitis can develop. The symptoms are pain deep in the wrist, a weakness in the thumb or hand, or soreness when you move your thumb.

Carpal Tunnel Syndrome

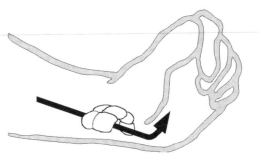

Carpal Tunnel Syndrome can have serious consequences if it is untreated and becomes chronic. One of the hand's major nerves passes through the tunnel formed by the rough "U" shape of the small carpal bones and is held in place by the carpal tendon which runs across the open side.

Pressure from swelling or repetitive motion can compress this nerve and cause severe pain in the hand, wrist, and forearm. A characteristic numbness in the thumb and first two fingers is often the first sign of the beginnings of Carpal Tunnel Syndrome. If there is general numbness in the hand or all the fingers, Thoracic Outlet Syndrome is a more likely culprit. The chapter on the upper back on page 117 will tell you more about that.

Carpal Tunnel Syndrome, in its early stages, can be helped using the suggestions in this chapter. Rest and splinting with a wrist brace are the first steps. If it occurs during the later stages of pregnancy, it often clears up as the extra fluid disappears. More severe cases may require surgery, but this is a last resort. It should be considered after careful consultation with your health care practitioner and after you are both sure that your condition is not caused by continued swelling, Thoracic Outlet Syndrome, or compression of the nerve somewhere else in your arm.

You use the cradle grip all day long, so...

shift that load!

Alternate sides whenever possible. You can let both arms and both sides of your trunk share some of the work. If you've gotten a long phone call? "Hold on a minute, please," until you can make yourself comfortable. Arrange your baby in a way that protects your wrist. Or get someone to help. All too often we can't or won't ask for help until we disable ourselves. Then we do get help, because we can't do any more. But why wait until you're in pain? Ask first!

Massage

Soreness and swelling can both be relieved with gentle massage.

If swelling is your main problem, begin your massage at your fingers and then work back toward your elbow. Stroke firmly (you could think of it as milking). Finish up by holding your hand above your head for a few minutes. This will allow the excess fluid to drain away from the swollen area. Your body will eliminate it later.

To relieve muscle aches and cramping in your wrist, work from the elbow toward the hand. Imagine you are moving the pain away from yourself and throwing it off.

You can also touch the insides of your wrists together and roll and rub them back and forth. This massage is pleasant and you'll stretch and exercise exactly the right muscles at the same time.

TIP (for working parents): Keyboard hand position and tension causes many sore wrists. This can happen in any occupation such as checkout clerk, cashier, or assembly line operator where a single hand or forearm motion is repeated many times.

Use the exercises and massages in this section as often as possible during your work day.

Exercises and Stretches

No exercise will completely eliminate the danger to your wrists, but these will reduce your risk and help you to prevent further injuries.

The Bag Lift

This will strengthen the extending muscles. Rest your arm on a table so that your hand and wrist extend beyond the edge. Your palm should face the floor. Hold a hand bag or a shopping bag with something light in it by the handle and lift it up. Do this three times a day with six repetitions each time. As you build up strength, increase the weight of the bag by adding a soup can or two.

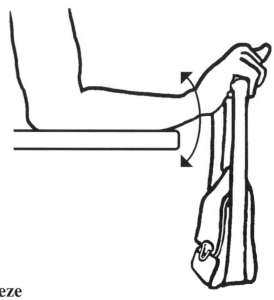

The Squeeze

Squeeze a soft rubber or foam ball or a big sponge. This strengthens the forearm muscles. The squeeze and release action will pump some of the excess fluid out of the wrist and reduce the pressure on tendons, arteries, and nerves.

Cool Relief

Running cold water over your wrist will bring some relief for the problem of excess fluid (It's also great on hot summer nights). The cold constricts your blood vessels and reduces the amount of fluid passing into the tissues around the wrist. Cold applications also relieve discomfort.

TIP: The string game, Cat's Cradle, is an excellent wrist conditioner.

The Wave

This exercise strengthens the wrist extensors, stretches the flexors, and, at the same time, it limbers up your neck. As you turn your head, keep your eyes parallel with the ground.

Raise one arm to the side with fingers pointing out and palm down. Look along your arm.

Extend your wrist (bend it up). Then, turn your head and look to the opposite side.

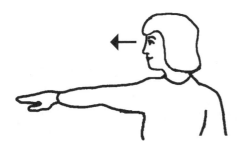

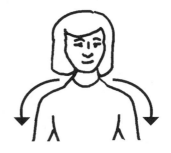

Raise the other arm and point your fingers up while lowering the first arm. Repeat.

Lower both arms to your sides. Shrug and let your shoulders relax.

A Leaning Stretch

Sit comfortably on a chair. Hold on to the sides with your finger tips. Tilt your head gently to the opposite side and then let your whole body lean slightly until you feel the stretch in your wrist. Repeat on the other side. This stretch will also benefit your neck.

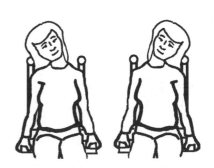

TIP: When you use the "cradle," hold something with the fingers of the lifting hand. You can grip the edge of your baby's blanket or a diaper wrap. This protects your wrist because you can't flex all the way when you grip something with your fingers.

Mechanical Support

A wrist brace is a mechanical help that can be useful when simple exercise and massage aren't sufficient.

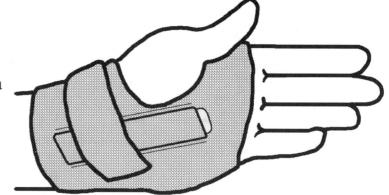

The brace gives support to the wrist and prevents you from moving it too far by holding it in a neutral position. It also eliminates some of the edema or swelling. Many of them have a removable insert that lets you control the amount of support and restraint.

Self-Adjustment

If some of the small carpal bones have been displaced, you can try this simple adjustment technique.

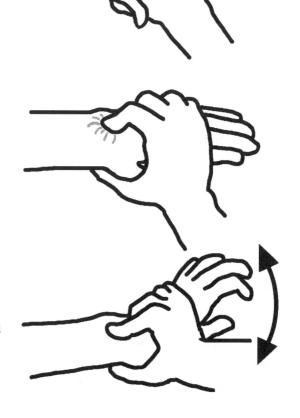

Grasp the hand on the arm with the sore wrist with your other hand and pull gently out toward the finger tips.

You will feel a shallow dip in the center of the upper surface of the affected wrist. Place the tip of your index or middle finger in this. Grasp the underside with your thumb.

Gently bend your hand up and down. If you are able to successfully slip the bone back into place, you will feel it "click."

• NURSING NOTE •

If you use only the cradling position when you nurse or bottle feed, you may develop a sore wrist, particularly if you tend to hold your baby on one side. Remember that the most important thing you can do for yourself (and your wrist) is to do things in different ways. For example, you can use a pillow under your arm to support your baby rather than carry the full weight with your wrist.

Or you can lie on your side. In this position a pillow will bring your baby closer without straining your wrist. This can also be used with bottle feedings.

If you breastfeed, try bringing your baby close, belly to belly, some of the time. You won't have to cock your wrist because you're supporting your baby with the flat of your hand and you're not supporting as much weight.

Do cradle your baby some of the time. Just make it one of the ways in which you feed your baby instead of the only way.

TIP: Good muscle balance is the best wrist protection. Whenever you flex your wrist to carry or cradle, remember to extend it afterwards.

Breast Pumps and Wrists

Some manual breast pumps use a cylindrical sleeve for the pumping action. Pumping with these can be a cause of wrist strain. Try holding the sleeve from below with your palm up and your elbow close into your side (imagine you're a singer and dancer and the pump sleeve is your cane). Use the motion of your whole arm for pumping. This protects your elbow as well as your wrist.

If pumping still bothers your wrist, several kinds of small electrical (battery or plug-in) pumps are available for rental or purchase and will solve this problem.

• LIFTING NOTE •

Hold your baby close when lifting. This gets the larger muscles of the back, shoulders, and trunk doing the work— and they do it better than your wrists!

A Last Word

Always do things in different ways. No single lifting technique is perfect. Bringing things close protects your wrists, but it can strain your knees. Vary your actions to strengthen and stretch yourself as you raise your child, rather than stress and wreck yourself by getting into a rut.

The "suitcase" grip is a strong grip that's easy on the wrist. Most children balk at being carried like a bag, although....

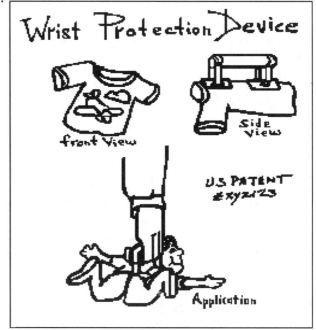

A Look Inside: The Wrist

Your wrist is a busy intersection for tendons, nerves, and arteries. It's another part of your body that you probably don't devote a moment's thought to until your hands are numb and tingling, or your wrist hurts!

Get acquainted with your wrist by first making a mental picture of your whole arm. Visualize the thick heavy muscles of the shoulder and upper arm. They taper down into the long muscles of the forearm and pass into the thin strong ones that control the movements of your fingers. All of the energy that can be brought to bear on your hand passes through the narrow channel of the wrist.

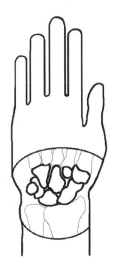

The wrist joint is made up of eight small bones, the carpals. These pebble shaped carpals connect the two long bones of the forearm with your finger bones. They allow the subtle movements used to clean a child's eye and the stronger movements needed for diapering a reluctant toddler.

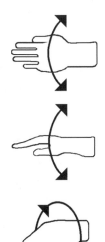

The wrist enables the hand to be moved up, down, and from side to side. By combining these, the hand can turn in a circle.

The extra fluid in your body during and just after pregnancy makes your wrist unusually vulnerable and the physical demands of parenting, particularly lifting and carrying your baby, can cause strain. However, most wrist problems will clear up with rest, exercise, and by your performing normal activities with care.

The Knee
(the in-between, back and forth joint)

COMMON PROBLEMS

It's not surprising that new mothers experience knee problems. Your knees were already under stress from pregnancy's postural changes. When you add the hormonal loosening (during and after pregnancy and during your period) of the thick ligaments that connect the bones in your knee, you can see that injury is even more likely. Of course, parenting, with all the extra kneeling and lifting, adds more stress.

The knee works like a simple hinge as it swings the lower leg back and forth. It doesn't allow for much twisting and turning; these motions usually come from the hips or the ankles and feet. When sideways movements don't come from these more flexible parts of your body, the knee is forced to do the twisting and winds up doing the aching.

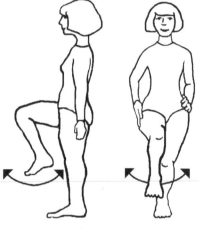

If you raise your leg in front of you with the knee bent and move it around you'll experience this for yourself. When you move back and forth the knee can move alone. When you move from side to side, the movement comes from the hip and you can feel it with your hand.

The knee is intimately connected by bands of muscle and tendon to your sacroiliac and your lumbar spine. Problems in those places can echo in your knees. Chronic knee problems (unless they are the result of a traumatic injury) often come from stiffness in the muscles around the hip. Many new–parent knee pains come from stiffness or stress in the muscles here. If you are having knee problems, read the hip chapter on page 98 next. Flattened arches can also cause knee problems. They pull the leg and knee inwards and this stresses muscles. Read about the feet on page 143.

> **TIP:** Some leg cramps are also caused by changes in your posture. During pregnancy your weight shifts forward over your toes and the muscles in your calves work harder to maintain your balance. With a new baby you also do a lot of carrying in front of you and this has the same effect. You can help yourself by occasionally shifting back onto your heels during the day and by massaging calves and feet at bedtime.

The Muscles Around the Knee

Two sets of muscles connect the pelvis to the knee. The quadriceps at the front of your upper leg and the hamstrings at the back. They attach to the bones around your knees and have a major effect on them. You can see why problems with these muscles have a direct effect on your knees.

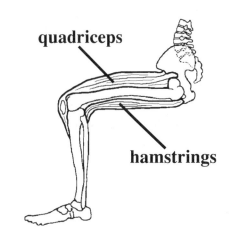

quadriceps

hamstrings

The Hamstrings

The upper hamstrings are muscles that begin at the bottom back of your pelvis at the ischial tuberosity (your 'sit' bone). They pass down the back of the upper leg and attach at the sides of the lower leg just below the knee. They pull the lower leg up and back and pull the whole leg back at the end of the swing of your forward stride.

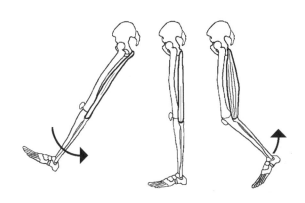

The Quadriceps

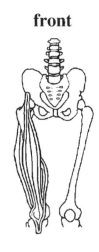

front

The quadriceps is actually a set of four muscles. They straighten your knee and swing your leg forward from the hip. All four merge in a tendon that surrounds and attaches to the kneecap before securing everything to the front of the lower leg. Many knee problems are the result of either weakness or tightness in the quadriceps. If you keep the quadriceps strong and flexible, you'll be doing a lot to keep your knees healthy.

TIP: If you have severely sprained your ankle, the same accident may have pushed the fibula (the smaller of the two bones in your lower leg) out of place. This can cause a sharp pinching sensation around the ankle and, sometimes, knee pain. Consult a physical therapist, podiatrist, orthopedist, or chiropractor if you suspect this is your problem.

Leg Swings

Since your knees take the stress when tight or weak muscles in the hips restrict your flexibility, keeping your hip joints moving freely will save your knees.

Stand on one leg and raise the other slightly off the floor and a little to the front. Let your leg relax and swing your foot from side to side. If you push your fingers deeply into the center of your buttock, you can feel the hip joint moving as you swing your foot.

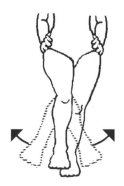

Stretching the Ankles and Feet

The feet and ankles, like the hips, move easily in more directions than the knees and tightness here can also create stress. Here are two stretches that will keep you limber at the bottom end and help protect your knees.

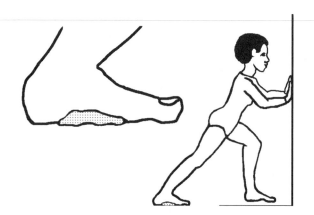

Lean into a wall from about three feet away. Bring one foot forward and bend that leg at the knee until you feel a stretch along the back of the straight leg. Place a sock or wash cloth under the arch of the back foot. This will stretch the calf muscles as well as the foot. Relax into this stretch and then reverse your legs to stretch the other side.

Next, simply point your toes so that your foot is sticking straight out, then curl your toes under. This will stretch the top of your foot and the front of your ankles. You can do this one standing, sitting, or lying down.

> **TIP (for working parents):** If your occupation requires you to sit a lot, the muscles around your hips can tighten up and contribute to stress at the knee. Be sure to sneak in time for some stretches.

Massage

You can give yourself a pleasant massage by rolling a tennis ball, or one of similar size, along the muscles at the outside of your thighs. Try rolling lengthwise as well as side to side. Then use the ball to massage the sides and backs of your calves. Give your knee cap a wiggle while you're at it.

LIFTING NOTE

Lifting heavy (and sometimes reluctant) young people puts a strain on more than just the lower back. Knee problems can often flare up in the years when you are caring for infants and toddlers.

There are no magic solutions, but there are several things you can do. First, and most important, use the exercises that strengthen and stretch your feet, ankles, hips and upper legs. Second, pay attention to what you are doing as you lift. Do you always lift in the same way? Notice what you do and then try some changes.

Sometimes a small change in the way you lift will make a big difference. Where are your feet when you lift something heavy? Do your toes generally point in or out? Try shifting your foot position, but don't be extreme, make changes slowly.

When your child can climb, find a foot stool or two-step step ladder and keep it near your changing table. Getting them to use it is no problem. They'll be proud of their ability and your knees (and lower back) will thank you.

A LAST WORD

Leaning and reaching too far forward sometimes causes knee pain, particularly if you are stiff in the hips or holding yourself tensely because of lower back pain. Changing a bed is an example of this. Try different ways to do the job without forcing your knees into awkward positions.

A Look Inside: The Knee

The knees work hard. They propel you forward, allow you to bend, stoop, squat, and, of course, kneel. While this is going on, they are also supporting the entire weight of your body and, during pregnancy, your baby's, too. Since the knee works as a simple hinge, it moves back and forth well, but is easily strained by twisting and turning.

Although the knee joint acts like a simple hinge, it is actually a combination of three joints. The two bones of the lower leg (tibia and fibula) connect to make one joint, they connect with the long upper leg bone (femur) to make another, and that connects with the kneecap.

Knee problems that involve the joint itself should be evaluated by a health care practitioner to determine which part of these joints needs attention, if you are to have successful treatment.

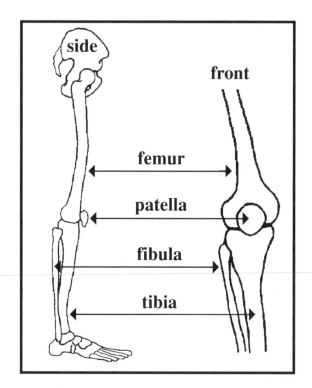

The kneecap or patella is a small, separate bone which has a dual role. It protects the front of the joint and contributes to the strength of the powerful quadriceps muscle.

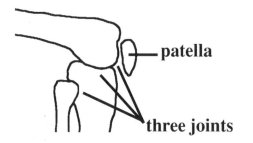

The powerful muscles of the upper and lower leg cross over each other at the knee and surround it with strong ligaments. Like other joints in your body, it's more vulnerable during and just after pregnancy and during the time of your period because of hormonal loosening.

TIP: The best way to keep your knees healthy is to keep the muscles at the hip stretched and strong and to make sure your feet (and, most importantly, your arches) are well supported with comfortable shoes.

Getting to the Bottom of Things
(your ankles and feet)

The Bad News

Your feet and your ankles have spent years supporting you and for nine months they have carried an ever increasing load. The weight of baby, amniotic fluid, and your own extra weight add thirty pounds or more to what they already supported. With the additional stresses of parenting, they may start to complain. If they complained before, they're probably shouting by now. Sprained ankles, flattened arches, and even broken bones in the feet are not uncommon for women in the last few months of pregnancy and the early months of the post-partum period.

Extra weight isn't the only cause of trouble. Changes in your posture also contribute to foot and ankle problems. Before pregnancy, much of your weight rests on the backs of the feet where the bones are thicker and well padded. As your baby grows, the new weight tips you forward. The toes and the ball of the foot work harder and aches and pains in those parts of your foot become common. The changes in how you walk (or waddle, in those last weeks) produce more strains as well as some of those unpleasant calf cramps at the end of the day.

After the birth, your body often continues to compensate for weight that's no longer there. You may feel like you're falling at times when you know you're really not! Balance is difficult and the unsteadiness can lead to the twisting missteps that cause strains and sprains of the ankle.

Regular old abuse and neglect also account for some of the problems you may experience. Most of us don't pay much attention to our feet. We jam and cram them into all kinds of shoes, force them to tilt at strange angles for the sake of a look, and generally ignore them. Child bearing will make any old foot problem worse.

The Good News

The good news is that almost all of these problems have solutions. Simple exercises and gentle massages for your ankles and feet (along with some care and thought about your shoes) will start your recovery. You will heal, and, if you take charge of your healing, you will come out ahead. For chronic problems, don't rely on self-treatment. Consult with your health care practitioner or a podiatrist, a doctor who specializes in feet.

What To Watch Out For

Because the main job of your legs and feet is walking, the ankles are strongest in front to back motion. It's the side to side weakness that's the biggest danger to your ankles during and after pregnancy, making ankle strains and sprains more likely.

Toes are much more than the ten little things that stick off the ends of your feet. Your toes help you sense balance and movement. They are a major part of your stride, and can be a major source of pain. Because your feet grow and spread out slightly during pregnancy, your old shoes may be too tight and may cause painful problems.

Too Short

Shoes that aren't long enough can deform your toes. Below are some examples of how the three bones in the toe can be pushed out of shape by shoes that are too short.

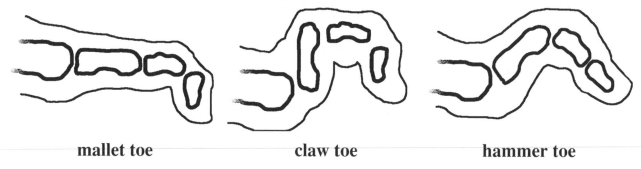

mallet toe   claw toe   hammer toe

Too Narrow

Hallux valgus is a deformation of the big toe caused by flat feet and narrow shoes. It is a frequent problem for women in their thirties or older. Your arch flattens over time and your stride (how you step) changes. You will tend to roll slightly over the inside of your foot and this forces the big toe toward the outside. Add tight shoes and the toe will become chronically bent with a bunion appearing on the pressured side.

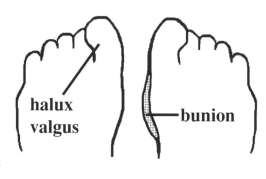

halux valgus   bunion

Soft Tissue Issues

Corns and bunions are symptoms of a deteriorating relationship between you and your shoes. Corns are the toe equivalent of a callus, bunions are more serious and reflect changes in the bone beneath the skin. Both can be treated, but until you find footwear that soothes and suits your feet, they will reappear.

For Toes and Feet - Shoes That Fit

Your foot size and shape change dramatically during the child bearing years. You can expect an increase of at least one-half size. The extra weight and hormonal loosening of ligaments during pregnancy will cause your arches to flatten and your feet to become longer and wider. New shoes should reflect these changes.

Your old shoes will probably be too short and too narrow. The squeeze of tight shoes can cause problems; corns, calluses, and blisters are the least of these. Toe deformities are more serious. Unless treated, these can become permanent deformities that will seriously affect your balance, comfort, and ability to walk.

Buying the Right Size Shoe

Always stand when having your feet measured. When your weight is resting naturally on your feet, your feet will be at the correct width. Your feet expand when they carry weight, so sitting measurements will result in shoes that are too narrow. Adequate length in your shoes is crucial, if you wish to avoid toe deformities.

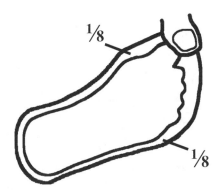

There should be a thumb nail's width between your longest toe (for some people the big toe, for others the second toe) and the front of the shoe.

Side width is also important. Allow ⅛ inch to ¼ inch extra on either side of the widest part of your foot for a good fit. This will help prevent some toe deformities, bunions, corns and calluses.

TIP: If bunions or toe deformations are a chronic problem for you, it would be wise to consult with a podiatrist, a doctor specializing in feet.

Put Comfort First

Sneakers with an arch support and lots of padding under the foot are generally the best shoe for all around use. If you have a choice, select sneakers with the most fabric and least cross strapping on the uppers. These will expand and be more forgiving of your changing feet.

Padding and Support

Baby your feet! Even if your old shoes seem comfortable, add foam insoles and arch supports (but only if your shoe is big enough to accommodate them). You'll find these in shoe, drug, and athletic supply stores. Extra padding to cushion your feet and extra support under your arches will make a big difference in how you feel.

Orthotics are custom made inserts for your shoes. If you have chronic problems or are severely uncomfortable, they are worth the expense. A podiatrist, physical therapist, orthopedist, or chiropractor will make a cast from the bottom of your foot and then have an orthotic made that exactly suits your needs.

> **TIP: The most important thing you can do for your toes (and the rest of your feet) is to invest in comfortable shoes that support you well.**

Foot Exercises and Stretches

The next three exercises can be done sitting down. They require simple props, a tennis ball (or slightly smaller), a towel, and some small toys (marbles are great).

Ball Rolling

This is a cross between exercise and massage. Rest your foot on top of the ball and roll it back and forth and side to side. Concentrate especially on the ball of the foot, letting the toes curl over and grip at the ball. Use whatever pressure feels best. You can do this either sitting or standing. Sitting is usually more comfortable.

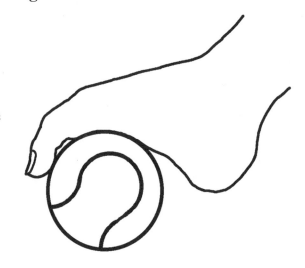

This exercise can sometimes readjust misaligned bones, particularly under the ball of the foot.

Towel Grabbing

Start with a towel spread out flat and with your toes over the nearest edge. Use your toes to grip and bunch the towel towards you. Do this as often as you like. It is particularly good for mallet, hammer, and claw toe problems since the grip and release movement help work the joints back into place and the exercise maintains the arch.

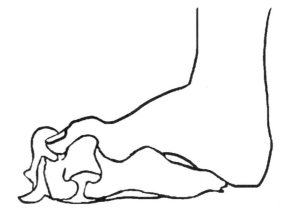

Toy Picking

If you have an older child at home, marbles, little plastic blocks, or small cars are perfect for picking up with your toes. Use both feet and give all of your toes a chance, not just the first two.

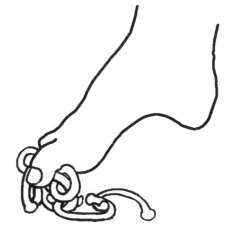

Weight Shifting

When you get up in the morning, stand with your feet squarely under you and slowly shift your weight forward and back. Move up onto your toes and back onto your heels a few times.

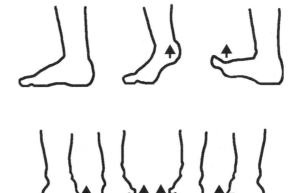

Try shifting from side to side and then do front and back again. Find a place in the middle that feels right. This will give you a comfortable stance that is balanced and equally distributed over both feet.

TIP: Keep a towel or a ball for foot exercises near your TV or your favorite spot for feeding your baby. Use them often.

Foot Massage

There is a kind of magic healing in the human touch. That's why a massage is a great gift. Have someone give you one. If no one's available, give yourself a treat. Special massage oils are not necessary, but since the feet tend to be rougher, at least on the bottom, oil makes for a smoother rub. If swelling still bothers you, end the massage by elevating your feet above the level of your hips for a few minutes.

How To Massage Your Feet

Begin with your neediest foot. Slide a finger between the toes, one pair at a time, and gently spread them apart. Then slide four fingers between all the toes on one foot and ease them back.

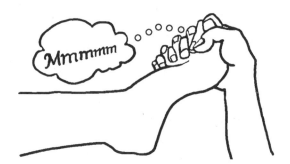

Stroke between the bones of the foot that run from ankle to toes. Do this on both sides of the foot. Rub deeply with a knuckle in the deeper places across the ball of the foot and in the heel.

Use your knuckles to press and deeply stroke first along the length of the arches and then from side to side. If there are sore spots, work on them a little.

Wind up by giving each toe a gentle rub and pulling it gently straight out. Repeat for the other foot.

Reflexology

Reflexology is a gentle healing art that uses pressure and massage on various spots on the soles of the feet. Each spot is supposed to correspond to another part of your body. Whether or not you believe in the system, it's a wonderful excuse for a foot massage. Have your partner read up on reflexology and practice on your feet.

> **CAUTION:** If you are pregnant, don't massage the area in back of your ankle bones and above the heel or the area four inches above the inner ankle bone. The traditional acupuncture points for bringing on labor are in these areas and should be avoided.

Sprained Ankle

Ankles are a frequent source of pain for pregnant and new mothers. Extra weight, the inability to see what's directly in front of your feet, and thinking about other things all lead to the missteps that strain and sprain.

Once an ankle is injured, it is four or five times more likely to be injured again unless you strengthen it correctly. If you strain or sprain your ankle, please take the time to let it heal thoroughly and make it strong.

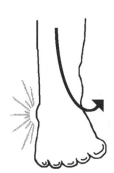

Almost all sprained ankles happen when the foot is suddenly turned too far to the inside. The damage is done to the muscles and ligaments on the outside of the ankle when they are suddenly and violently overstretched. Sprained ankles, where the ligaments connecting muscle to bone are damaged, often reoccur unless you spend the time to strengthen the muscles supporting your ankle.

CAUTION: Treat a sprained ankle quickly and completely. Use ice to reduce the swelling and continue ice treatments until the swelling is completely gone (the First Aid chapter on page 157 explains how). This may take longer than the first twenty-four hours. Use an elastic wrap to compress and stabilize your ankle for up to ten days.

Ankle Exercises and Stretches

Begin exercises to strengthen your ankle from seven to ten days after a sprain.

Ankle Circling

Lie on your back and prop your legs up so that they're comfortably supported straight in front of you. Make circles in the air with your feet. Do this for at least three minutes. You can also turn them from side to side as well as forward and back. This is a good exercise to do when you first wake up. Scoot down in the bed so your feet stick out over the end and rotate away.

Toe Lifting

The best exercise for building up the outside muscles (and stretching the inner muscles) is this:

Sit or lie with your leg supported on a pillow or bolster so that your foot is off the floor. Bring your foot up and out. Imagine stepping on the gas pedal of your car and then do the opposite. As you pull back, lead with the outside edge of your foot. Try for one hundred times a day. It doesn't really take all that long and it's well worth it, particularly if you've already had a strained or sprained ankle.

As soon as you can, add resistance to build strength. You can put a small, heavy pillow or a saggy handbag over your foot, or you can catch one end of an elastic loop (a giant rubber band, sewing elastic, or something similar) over your foot and the other end under a chair or table leg.

> **CAUTION: If you experience a sharp pinching feeling, see a physical therapist, podiatrist, orthopedist or chiropractor. Sometimes the fibula, one of the two bones in the lower leg, may pulled out of place by the same accident that sprained your ankle and may be causing this sensation.**

Foot Exercises for Ankles

All of the foot exercises are good for your ankles. If you are recovering from a sprained ankle, be cautious with the side to side shifting exercise. You can do it, but if it hurts or feels unstable, wait until you've healed and built up some strength.

A Last Word

You (and your feet) deserve the comfort and support of good fitting shoes.

A Look Inside: The Ankles and Feet

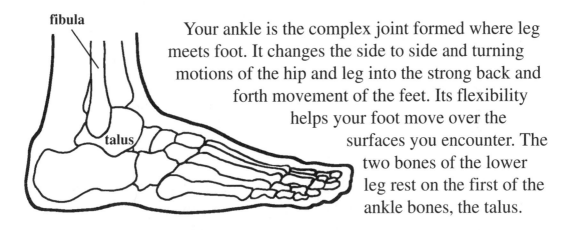

Your ankle is the complex joint formed where leg meets foot. It changes the side to side and turning motions of the hip and leg into the strong back and forth movement of the feet. Its flexibility helps your foot move over the surfaces you encounter. The two bones of the lower leg rest on the first of the ankle bones, the talus.

The changes in your balance and weight make pregnancy and the early post-partum period hard on your ankles and feet. For nine months your weight slowly shifted forward over the balls of your feet. Then, in the space of a few hours your center of gravity changed completely (along with everything else)!

The twenty eight small bones of the feet and the tough layers of muscle and ligament carry your weight and act as levers, pivots, and platforms for everything from ballet dancing and basketball to parenting.

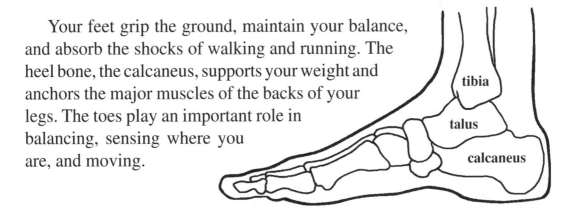

Your feet grip the ground, maintain your balance, and absorb the shocks of walking and running. The heel bone, the calcaneus, supports your weight and anchors the major muscles of the backs of your legs. The toes play an important role in balancing, sensing where you are, and moving.

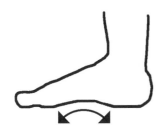

The bones of the mid-foot make two arches, from front to back and from side to side. These act as springs to carry your weight and strengthen the action of your toes as you walk.

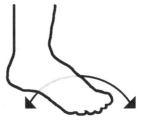

Putting It All Together
(the knee bone connected to the thigh bone...and everything else!)

What You've Learned So Far

When you think about all of its separate pieces, you can lose sight of your body's essential unity and balance. All the separate bones, ligaments, and muscles are part of a whole, and all of the parts balance and work together.

Interconnection

Interconnection means more than just your joints linking one bone to another. The muscles, ligaments, and tendons in your body overlap and support one another in such a way that what happens in one place echoes in many other places. Interconnection is a characteristic of your whole body. Your hormonal system links your reproductive cycle, your mood, and the tautness of your ligaments. What you eat and drink has an effect on how well your body works and on your feeling of well being. When you are aware of all these connections, the idea of balance makes good sense.

Balance

The balanced nature of our bodies starts with the breath (in and out), and extends to muscles (extending and flexing, adducting and abducting), and to our posture (if part of us sticks out in front, some other part sticks out in back to keep us from falling over). And don't forget the balance that you have to consciously maintain, balancing activities left and right, front and back, and the vital balance between rest and activity.

Finally,

A new parent's life is blissful but, at times, physically hard. You come into this period in your life with new stresses plus old problems and habits (you stand more on one foot, favor one hand, or tip your head more to one side than the other). Together these can intensify old problems or make you vulnerable to new ones. None of this is hopeless and the solutions don't require heroic efforts, enormous strength, or the flexibility of a contortionist.

It Takes Just Three Things

Becoming aware of your body.

Using gentle, balanced motion in all that you do.

Spending time on yourself.

First Aid: Acute Injuries
(from time of injury to three days)

"RICE"

Rice is the word to remember. It stands for the first four things to do for a muscular injury. You will find out how in the following chapters.

Rest
- Stay off or do not use injured area.
- Place the injury (and yourself) in a comfortable position.

Ice
- Apply cold: either ice packs or compresses
- Use for short, regular periods (see page 157)

Compress
- Quickly apply moderate pressure over the area.
- Use cautiously (see page 158)

Elevate
- Combine with rest.
- If possible, place the injury above the level of your heart.

Seek Medical Help

If your injury incapacitates you, worries you, or affects your neck, spine, or hurts enough to limit your ordinary activites, seek the immediate assistance of your health care provider. She or he can provide you with a preliminary diagnosis and additional aids for acute injuries. These may include:

- Tests to determine the severity of injury.

- Stabilization.

- Pain and swelling reduction.

- Healing exercises and stretches.

- Medication

CAUTION: If your are pregnant or nursing a baby, be sure to inform your health care practitioner before taking any tests or medications.

First Aid: Sub-Acute Injuries
(from three days to four to six weeks)

Rest
Rest is important, but movement is essential to the proper healing of muscular injuries once you're over the acute stage. Consult with your physician, chiropractor, or a physical therapist to find out what kind of movement is appropriate for you.

Cold or hot
If swelling and pain is present, continue the use of ice. If the swelling has gone down, heat can relax muscles and improve circulation. This will reduce aching. Don't use heat for longer than thirty minutes at a time, however.

Contrasting Hot and Cold
Alternating hot and cold is beneficial, especially if the swelling persists.

Massage
Massage relaxes muscles and improves the circulation to injured parts. This will speed the healing process.

Exercise
Use gentle exercise to begin to go beyond the painful range of motion. This protects against developing compensatory injuries, such as a stiff neck when you've injured your lower back. It also relieves tightness and stiffness in the healing muscles.

Medical Help
This includes tests, medication, and forms of treatment such as ultrasound and electrical muscle stimulation that are available only through qualified health care providers.

You will find specific information about all of these beginning on page 157.

TIP ABOUT MUSCLE PAIN: Soreness or pain from a pulled muscle should diminish in ten days and complete healing should take place in four to six weeks. If it is taking longer, then there is probably something more complicated happening and you should consult your health care practitioner, if you haven't already. Don't suffer, seek help.

First Aid: Chronic Injuries
(lasting more than six weeks or reoccurring)

> **HOT OR COLD?: If it stings, stabs, burns, or begins to swell - use ice.
> If it aches, throbs, or just feels sore - heat.**

Ice

Use longer applications, up to twenty minutes, but heed the cautions on page 157.

Heat

Use heat if you find that it helps to reduce aching in the muscles.

Medical Help

It is particularly important to shop around for a health care provider who will support you with his or her expertise and teach you how to begin healing yourself over the long term. You need to find out why your injury is not getting better and what are the causes. With that information it will be possible to develop exercise and stretching programs that will both protect and heal you. This book will help you work out ways of safely doing everyday things.

Chronic injuries usually mean chronic pain. Many hospitals now support clinics or groups that assist people with chronic pain and these have proved helpful to many. There are a variety of techniques to relieve pain and its causes; you'll find them and, we hope, relief on page 167.

Stretching and Strengthening

The back, ankles, and wrists are sites of common recurrent injuries. The risks of reinjury can be reduced and healing speeded by exercises that develop the strength of supporting muscles and by stretches that increase your flexibility. You will find both in this book. Strengthening and stretching are often needed for the part of your body opposite the part of you that's in pain. The best exercises for chronic back problems are those that strengthen the abdominal muscles. The best stretches for mid-back problems are those that loosen up the muscles of the chest.

> **TIP: <u>STRAIN OR SPRAIN?</u> Nobody ever remembers the difference! For first aid, it doesn't matter. At the time of injury, treat them exactly the same. (A strain is an injury to muscle or tendon, a sprain is an injury to the ligaments that hold bones together. Sprains take longer to heal.)**

First Aid: How To Do It
(the three reduces)

> **The general principles for first aid treatment of muscular injury.**

Reduce The Risk of Further Injury

When you suffer a muscular injury, don't put off treating it. Immediately begin the "RICE" treatment. If necessary, immobilize the injured part of your body. Professional materials are not necessary. It's easy to improvise with ordinary household items. For example, the curved side of a plastic ice cream container can be cut to size and fitted within the palm and fingers to splint a sprained finger.

Reduce Swelling

Swelling is a result of the body's quick, protective reaction to injuries. When tissue is damaged and the skin is broken, it makes good sense for your body to flood the area. It speeds up the delivery of nutriments, blood clotting factors, and the white blood cells that fight infection. Extra fluids also help flush out unwanted materials. Unfortunately, when the skin is not broken the excess fluid is trapped and it takes some time to drain away. During this time the swelling causes pressure and pain, limits your ability to move, and prevents the muscles from functioning properly. Swelling is particularly troublesome around joints. Prolonged swelling (a week or more) may lead to permanent changes such as muscle adhesions, compression of blood vessels, and loss of sensation.

Reducing the swelling in muscular and joint injuries will reduce pain and speed healing. You will recover the use of the injured part of your body more quickly.

Reduce Pain

Anything that you can do to alleviate the pain will help to reduce muscle spasms. This decreases the amount of future aching and soreness. Resting, ice, pain killers, homeopathic remedies, compression, massage, ultrasound, and acupuncture are all possible choices. Resting the injured area and, if possible, your whole self is the first and most important thing to be done.

> **CAUTION:If you are nursing or are pregnant, some methods and remedies are not appropriate for you and your baby. Make sure your health care provider knows about your condition and your needs.You will find more specific information at the end of the chapter.**

First Aid: Methods
(how to do it)

Rest

Rest means not using the injured part of your body and making it (and yourself) as comfortable as possible. You may want to keep a knee or finger slightly bent, or rest your shoulder by keeping your arm at your side.

Ice and Cold Applications

Cold can be used for all acute injuries. Apply it five or six times a day for ten minutes during the first three or four days. After that, use it three or four times a day. If there is any swelling, continue to use ice.

Cold can be used at any time. It does not have to be used just in the first twenty-four hours. For some chronic lumbar, sacroiliac, and ankle problems, ice is the only way to handle the pain. Ice does so much that it would qualify as a wonder drug, if it wasn't so cheap.

Ice works as a pain killer by reducing the pain signals sent by the nerves in the skin and soft tissue. It slows down the speed of nerve conduction and this reduces the spasms that often occur in injured muscles. It also constricts the blood vessels and limits the excess swelling.

If ice is left on for more than about twenty minutes, it will dilate the blood vessels as heat does and the area will start to feel warmer. This makes it effective for chronic injuries. For acute injuries where you only want constriction, limit the application to ten minutes or less.

CAUTION: Ice placed directly on the skin can be hazardous. Ice is a strong remedy and should be used with care. Follow these guidelines:

- **Direct, prolonged contact with the skin can cause frost bite or frost nip. Put a wet wash cloth over the injury and place the ice pack on top of that. Cover both with a towel or a loosely wrapped bandage.**

- **Don't apply cold over the kidneys, heart, or temples. Ice over the kidneys can cause urine retention, if the ureters contract. Ice placed directly over the heart may constrict the blood vessels serving the heart and cause aching. Ice over the temples can constrict the vessels carrying blood to the brain and cause dizziness or fainting.**

How To Apply Cold

Ice bags: Put cubes or crushed ice in a plastic bag or ice pack. Apply to the injured area for ten to fifteen minutes (but no longer) with a cloth between ice and skin.

Ice bucket: (for hand and foot injuries) Place ice cubes into a container large enough to accommodate the injured part and add enough water to cover. It becomes extremely cold and most people can last for only a few minutes. It is very effective .

Ice towels: Dunk a towel in an ice water bucket. Wring it out and apply to the injury. When it begins to warm up, dunk it again.

Ice massage: Freeze water in a small paper cup. When you need the ice, peel back the paper to expose an ice surface. Swirl it slowly over the injured part for three to five minutes. You can do this three to four times a day.

Commercial ice packs: These are convenient and mold easily around many body parts, but the quality is uneven. Some ice packs get too cold and others not cold enough. It can be cheaper and more reliable to use plain old ice. If you do use commercial packs, avoid direct contact with your skin. Wrap them in a piece of cloth or paper towel.

Compression

Compression is a good way to limit the amount of excess fluid at the site of the injury and reduce swelling. In the early stages of an injury, it helps prevent further damage by limiting your movement.

You can use elastic bandages shaped to specific parts of your body (the ones that fit over knee, ankle, or whatever), two to six inch elastic bandages, splinting, surgical adhesive tape, compression stockings, or special appliances such as wrist splints.

Never use more than moderate pressure. Whatever you use should feel snug, but not tight or constricting. Be sure nothing is so tight that circulation is cut off. Always wrap a compression bandage in a spiral direction, not straight around any part of your body. This will protect your circulation.

Preformed elastic bandages are less bulky and easier to wear under clothing. If you use an ace bandage wrap, check it for sagging and wrinkling at regular intervals and rewrap it as necessary. Make sure, each time, not to wrap it too tightly.

Never leave compression wraps on for long periods of time. Don't wear them to bed at night. Lying on the wrapped area can cut off circulation and make things worse.

Elevation

Swelling can be painful. It limits movement and it can slow the healing process. Elevation helps reduce swelling that has already occurred. If possible, rest with the injured part of your body above the level of your heart. This will help drain extra fluid off using the force of gravity. If you combine elevation with simple, non-stress exercises, you can pump excess fluid away from an injury. Elevation also gives you a good excuse to rest the injured part.

Heat

Heat is a wonderful therapeutic tool. It relaxes muscles, soothes aches, and helps healing. Heat works by dilating the blood vessels. This speeds the circulation of blood to the injured area. Whenever muscles contract they are working hard and producing waste products. When injured muscles go into spasm, they are overworked. Large accumulations of these waste products cause the "aching feeling" in tired or injured muscles. An increased flow of blood helps the body flush the waste products away and promotes healing.

How To Apply Heat

Hydroculator pack: This is a commercial product that you can find in any drugstore. Each pack contains a gel that holds the heat absorbed when you place them in boiling water. They do require caution because they can become extremely hot. Wrap them in several layers of toweling before application; this will prevent blistering and burning. Moist heat in this form penetrates fairly well and reaches moderately deep aches and pains. Hydroculator packs come in a variety of sizes. Since they can be easily shaped, they are useful for a wide range of injury sites.

Microwave packs: These contain small pellets rather than a liquid gel and are easy to prepare. They also require caution because of the risk of too high a heat. Test before using and don't apply them directly to your skin.

Hot compresses: There are a number of compresses recommended by herbalists for sore and aching muscles. Grated ginger is a favored Chinese remedy. Generally they are applied with cloths that have been soaked in water boiled with the herbs and then wrung out. They are another form of moist heat and, whether or not they are more effective than plain moist heat, they certainly have pleasant and soothing smells and are fun to use.

Hot water bottles: The old fashioned hot water bottle is economical and easy to use. They aren't very flexible, but are good when you have a small area that requires heat. Psychologically, they are very nice to have tucked in at your feet on cool nights.

Heating pad: Heating pads are flexible and mold easily to body parts. They usually allow a choice of heat settings. Their big drawback is that they keep right on heating. If you forget about the time or fall asleep, you may be stiffer than when you started because the prolonged heat and increased blood flow will cause swelling. Lying on one for an extended period can cause uncomfortable burns. Use a heating pad for no more than twenty minutes and let a couple of hours pass before using it again. There is some controversy about using them if you are pregnant because of the possible effects of electrical fields on the developing fetus, so use with caution.

Massage: Gentle massage, perhaps with a soothing ointment, will generate warmth and ease tense muscles. However, gentle is the key word. Don't press or rub to the point of pain, particularly with new injuries.

Contrasting Hot and Cold

You can use any form of cold and alternate it with any form of hot. The contrast helps to pump the swelling out of the injured area as the blood vessels are first constricted and then dilated.

This is excellent therapy for subacute injuries because it promotes circulation and healing. Alternately apply cold and hot for one to two minutes each, four or five times at each session. You can do this three to four times a day. If you have a dunkable injury like a finger, wrist, or ankle you can use two buckets, one cold and one hot.

Therapeutic Ultrasound

This form of ultrasound is delivered at a different frequency from that used to provide an image of the baby inside the uterus. Therapeutic ultrasound is delivered in two different ways, pulsed and continuous. Continuous ultrasound is used to provide deep heat to injured tissues without burning the skin. In pulsed ultrasound the waves are delivered in bursts. This pumps fluid out of deeper tissues and reduces swelling, but doesn't heat them up.

Electrical Stimulation

Electrical stimulation can be applied to muscles to get them to relax. Electrical stimulation causes muscles to contract for longer than normal and fatigues them. It is most effective on deep or severely spasmed muscles which will not yield to massage.

Massage

The touch of a caring hand has its own special and ancient place in the art of healing. When massage is used around injuries, it must be gentle. When an injury causes swelling, it works best if the strokes are from the injury site back toward the heart. The massage will then be working with the body's natural drainage system, the lymphatics. The fluids will be finally excreted through the urinary system.

Later on, more vigorous or concentrated massage can be used. It can also be applied to scar tissues. Read about scar massage in the chapters on episiotomies and tearing and the cesarean section. Massage is particularly useful for chronic conditions.

Movement

Early gentle movement programs promote healing, improve alignment, and increase the function of the affected areas, and will leave you with fewer problems later on. Early movement is now considered the best form of treatment for most injuries, even the most severe. Extended periods of immobilization either in casts, restrictive appliances, garments, or beds have been found to slow down healing and create new problems such as chronic stiffness, contractures, or osteoporosis.

As soon as it's tolerable, you should begin weight-bearing activities with injured limbs and sore backs. It is important for you to begin moving both for your own feeling of independence and to get the healthy stresses of gravity and muscle contraction working for you.

Movement programs generally progress through a series of steps. The step at which you begin depends on the severity of your injury and should be determined by your health care provider, in most cases this will be a physical therapist.

• Passive: the injured part is moved for you by someone else.

• Active assistance: you move as much as you can and then are helped.

• Active: you use your own recovering muscles to move.

• Active Resistance: your muscles work against an outside force.

TENS Unit

"TENS" stands for Transcutaneous Electrical Nerve Stimulation. This is a simple, non-invasive way of controlling pain. The unit is about the size of a small pocket tape recorder. Small pads are connected to the TENS unit by wires and placed on the painful area. Non-painful electrical impulses are sent to the brain just ahead of the pain signals and this reduces the amount of muscle spasm and discomfort.

Pain Killers and Other Drugs

If you are nursing, you should be aware of the potential effects of all medicines, even old, familiar, over-the-counter drugs. Of the most common, acetaminophen and ibuprofen seem to be safe. Aspirin should be used cautiously. One useful rule of thumb is to avoid pain remedies that contain combinations of drugs. This will simplify any questions you have and make your life easier.

If you have any doubts or questions, seek advice. In almost all cases, you'll be able to relieve your pain and continue to breastfeed. Your druggist, pediatrician, and groups that support breastfeeding such as LaLeche League are all useful sources of information. Some hospitals will provide information on drugs and nursing, if you contact the pharmacy. Don't hesitate to ask and do be pushy. (More information about resources is on page 178).

Heat

Steam baths, saunas, and very hot baths should be avoided. The fetus is normally about ½ degree warmer than the mother and anything that interferes with your own ability to dissipate heat is potentially harmful to the fetus.

Ultrasound

Ultrasound used as a source of deep heat should be avoided on the back, pelvic area, and abdomen. It can heat up the fetus. The American Physical Therapy Association recommends against using ultrasound on these parts of the body during pregnancy. They feel that the transmission paths for heat in the body are not well enough understood and that it is better to avoid any risk to the developing baby.

Electrical Equipment

TENS, Electrical Muscle Stimulation, and any other equipment that either introduces electrical impulses into the mother's body or emits strong electrical fields should be used only with extreme caution and under the supervision of a heath care professional who is thoroughly informed about fetal development.

Medical Tests

X-rays, MRI, and CAT scans are tests that expose the mother and developing child to strong radiation of different kinds and should be avoided except when absolutely necessary for medical purposes and, even then, only under the closest supervision by specialists who are thoroughly informed about the risks to the baby.

Massage and Acupuncture

Avoid the backs and sides of ankles, the area on the inside of your shin, and just above the knee on the inside of the thigh. These areas contain points that are traditional places for stimulating labor.

Don't rub here, if you are pregnant.

Alternative or Wholistic Medications

If you are using alternative forms of medicine, use caution and make sure that you and your practitioner understand the contents and effects of any herbal teas, poltices, or other remedies on pregnancies, breastfeeding, and women's bodies. Be as cautious with alternative medicines as you would with those prescribed by Western medicine.

Seeking Professional Help

Healing from muscle, joint, and bone injuries takes time. It also requires cooperation between you and your health care provider, and cooperation between you and your body. Finding a health care practitioner who is going to help you heal from an immediate injury is a good idea. Finding one who is going to go beyond this and help you prevent future injuries is a wonderful idea. Sometimes this is hard.

Taking Charge of Your Own Healing

A health care practitioner should always be a partner in your recovery. Pick one who is going to help you do the healing. This may mean shopping around. When you are in pain, that isn't always easy. However, most people you see for first aid care will be able to treat the acute condition and give you time to make choices.

What To Look For

Here are some questions to help you evaluate your medical practitioner.

- **Does this person perform a thorough physical examination?** Nobody can make an complete assessment of your condition without a thorough, hands on, examination. This means looking at, touching, moving, and testing the injured area. If your foot is bothering you, you should be asked to take your socks off, if it's your back, then it's your shirt. No one can make an accurate diagnosis without an examination. It may also mean using appropriate diagnostic tests.

- **Does this person listen well?** What kind of questions does this person ask you? Is she or he curious about your medical history, the details of how you injured yourself, and your feelings about your present condition? This kind of information is necessary for understanding your injury and deciding on the best program for healing.

  You should be asked questions like:

  Has this happened before?

  In what positions is it worse, better?

  Does pain increase or decrease during the day or night?

  What work or home activities make it worse?

  Are you experiencing headaches or bladder or bowel changes?

- **Is this person a good teacher?** You will probably have gained some idea of this person's ability, background, and experience before your visit. The next clue is how well he or she can communicate. Does he or she make it easy for you to understand what has happened and what you can do about it?

- **Does this person intend to make you a partner in your healing?** Avoid anyone who promises an instant cure. Avoid anyone who intends to do it all for you. The first of these is impossible, the second, undesirable. Look for someone who will educate you. The only person who is finally going to insure your healing and recovery is you.

- **What do others say?** This doesn't need too much explanation. Ask around and be pushy. Use local resources and those listed at the back of this book.

- **Last, and most important, is there empathy for you as a new parent?** You won't always connect with someone who is a parent or who immediately understands your situation. On the practical level, your health care professional should know something about the safety of tests in relationship to your body, the safety of pain medications if you are nursing your infant, and the fluctuations and stress of pregnancy and delivery.

If you find someone who satisfies most of the requirements, but not this last one, feel free to educate him or her. Any health care professional who has met your other requirements is going to be eager to learn more.

Who Can Help?

Orthopedist: A medical doctor who specializes in bone and bone-related problems and has trained as a surgeon. An orthopedist can perform surgery, give X-rays prescribe medications, and order sophisticated tests.

Gynecologist: A medical doctor specializing in women's reproductive problems. She or he can perform surgery, prescribe medications, and order tests.

Uro-gynecologist: A medical doctor with specialized training in a women's urological problems. She or he can perform surgery, prescribe medications, and order tests. Urologists usually treat male urinary and reproductive problems.

Osteopath: A doctor trained in a medical system that emphasizes bones and the importance of the spine. Osteopaths often use natural homeopathic remedies. They can perform sophisticated tests.

Podiatrist: A doctor specializing in the foot and ankle. She or he is often the best source of help for foot injuries. Podiatrists can perform surgery on the feet, prescribe medications, order x-rays, provide foot supports and special shoes.

Chiropractor: A doctor trained in a system that puts a major emphasis on the manipulation of the spine. Chiropractors may use other techniques such as acupuncture, applied kinesthesiology, and massage. They can order x-rays, but cannot prescribe medications.

Physical Therapist: A practitioner specializing in the rehabilitation of the whole body through muscle strengthening, bone realignment, functional activities, and movement. In some states they are licensed as primary health care providers. In others, they receive referrals from doctors. They cannot prescribe medications or order x-rays.

Occupational Therapist: A practitioner specializing in rehabilitation through and for practical activities. They are particularly skilled in arm and hand activities, mental function, and neurological problems.

Certified Massage Therapist: A practitioner with at least six months to a year of formal training in massage. They cannot prescribe medications or diagnose dysfunctions. They are usually certified only by their own organization. There are also other body work systems such as Rolfing, Heller, and Polarity that use forms of touch and massage to encourage the body's natural healing process.

Wholistic Practitioners: There are many medical systems in the world, some of them far older than our own. Ayurvedic medicine from India and acupuncture from China are two of these. Homeopathy is a European system that was quite common in the United States through the beginning of the twentieth century. Many people have found these and other systems of health care to be beneficial. If you chose to take charge of your own healing and feel that traditional western medicine is not helpful, then explore them. Wholistic practitioners are not as closely regulated or regularly certified as western doctors. You will have to use your judgement carefully when choosing one.

Movement Systems: There are several systems of therapeutic movement that many people have found beneficial. The Alexander Technique and Feldenkrais are two of the better known. Their primary goal is to help people re-educate their bodies so that they can move well and without injury. Yoga is another form of exercise and movement that has been useful to many. If you are considering yoga, be very selective about the teacher you chose. Some vigorous forms of yoga and yoga that is taught inexpertly can do more harm than good for people with chronic problems.

And Last, But Not Least

Yourself: The most important health care practitioner of all. You can provide the three basic ingredients for all healing: rest, good nutrition, and appropriate exercise.

Pain

What Is Pain?

Each of us experiences pain in our own way. It is hard to define and often even harder to describe. We all know that pain is, well, painfully real. Scientists continue to explore the chemical and electrical components of our body's experience of pain. This knowledge has given us tools to relieve or reduce pain that range from powerful drugs to the application of minute electrical currents. There are also alternative ways of dealing with physical discomfort. Some of these ways may be useful as supplements to methods of pain relief you already use. Some may reduce or eliminate the need for stronger remedies.

Pain is a warning that something is wrong and needs to be tended to. For this reason you shouldn't deny pain and just tough it out. Heed the warning, even if all you do is slow down and listen to your body.

Is It All In My Head?

No. Pain is real. It is a basic part of our animal being, one that we share with all other creatures. It's purpose is to protect us from harm. And no matter what its origin, it points to something that needs attention. If your health care provider sees you as being weak or hysterical, this is no help at all. What you perceive as painful and how it affects you is all that is important. A responsible health care provider will make your experience of pain a part of her or his total diagnosis.

Is Some Of It In My Head?

Maybe. We all know that everyone experiences pain in different ways. One person may have a cavity filled without novacaine, while another would prefer to be totally unconscious. One person can't tolerate a cut finger and another is incapacitated by a sore muscle. What you describe as a dull ache might be excruciatingly painful to someone else. Pain is relative. Different people experience pain differently.

We also know that pain is relative for each individual person. We even experience the "same" pain differently under different conditions. Banging your shin on the edge of the bed will "feel" one way on a relaxed sunny morning as you get ready for a pleasant day. You just toss it off. Later in the afternoon when you're tired, racing to put clothes away, thinking about dinner, and the children are screaming, the same kind of injury may hurt a lot more.

Arrgh, This Is Making Me Tense

We do know that pain is increased by physical tension. This is one area where the relationship between your emotional feelings and your physical feelings is clear. People who suffer chronic pain or are afraid of re-injuring themselves need to be aware of this relationship. It can make their experience of pain easier or harder. Being in pain from an injury is bad enough; having the pain multiplied by emotional tension about the pain is horrible. If you find yourself in this category, pain management programs such as those now run by some hospitals can be very helpful.

Some Things Will INCREASE Your Pain

Your experience of pain can be magnified by many things. Fatigue, worries, old anxieties, food allergies, and caffeine stimulants are some of the things that can intensify your experience of pain. When you know this, you have a tool to control the pain of most muscular injuries. Pain should serve its warning function, but not dominate your life.

Some Things Will decrease Your Pain

Rest: The oldest and best of all remedies. All parents have a hard time getting enough and new parents find it the hardest. However, it should be first on your list of things to use for the treatment of pain.

A good cry: Emotional release is often overlooked as a method of pain reduction, but it is simple and very effective, particularly for new parents. Physical and emotional stress are a part of every new parent's life. Tensions can build and build until they spill over into physical discomfort. Don't hold back on your feelings. It's true, a good cry will make you feel better.

Cold packs and hot water bottles: Simple, around-the-house remedies can work wonders. The chapter on First Aid contains many useful suggestions. Simple remedies, simple comforts, and a good cuddle all help.

Shifting your attention: Easier said than done! But it can work wonders. Listening to a favorite song, changing tasks, taking a walk, calling a friend, or getting lost in a book can break the hold of an insistent ache or pain. You can stick notes up in key places that remind you to pause and relax.

Hypnosis: There's nothing magical about hypnosis. It's just a more specific way of shifting your attention. A professional hypnotist or psychologist can work with you to begin the process. Many people find that self-hyponosis is easy to learn and use.

Meditation: Another way to shift your attention. This one brings you from the world outside to the world inside. We often dismiss it as something from Eastern cultures that won't work for us, but meditation has an honorable history in all of the major religions of the world and has much to offer sufferers of physical pain.

Counseling: Some people find that pain has begun to take over their lives. If this happens to you, counseling from a social worker, a psychologist, priest, rabbi, minister, or peer can help put you back in charge.

Movement: Simple and appropriate physical exercise will aid healing, change your point of view, and restore your confidence in your body's recuperative powers. The body's natural opiates are released with exercise and exertion. A good workout or just a long walk can make you feel better.

Accupuncture: This is a traditional form of healing from China. It can be very helpful with certain kinds of pain and some of our pain relief technologies, such as the TENS unit, developed out of studies of this ancient medical art.

Nutrition: What we eat and drink affects how we feel. At no time in your life is this more true than during the post-partum period. The long work of growing the baby within you can deplete your body of essential vitamins and minerals. Pregnancy and childbirth place an enormous strain on your entire system. When your body is under this much stress, the affects of food allergies, sensitivites, or missing nutrients may be exaggerated. This will be reflected in increased sensitivity to pain and irritability. Eating well and drinking enough can make a big difference. Getting enough fluids is particularly important, even if it makes you urinate more frequently.

Hospital programs: Many hospitals have clinics and specialized programs to help people with pain, particularly chronic pain. They use combinations of some of the ideas recommended here and will help you develop a plan suited to your needs.

Self knowledge: Understanding what is going on with your body, how it works, and what you can do to help it all contribute to pain relief. The part of pain that is tied up with fear and dread is banished when you begin to understand your body and take charge of your healing.

A Last Word

Pain has a real warning function, but don't let it dominate your life.

Taking Care of Yourself

Planning the day

In the first days and weeks post-partum your baby will claim your time, your thoughts, your feelings, and your energy. This is the way it should be. Let everything else slide. If all you can do is take a shower, do a little food shopping, and make a phone call or two, that's great. New babies will fill up all the time that there is - and then some! It's smart and healthy to readjust your goals and plans for yourself, your partner, and your baby.

Think about the next day before you go to sleep. Be as realistic as you can about what needs to be done and what you have the time, energy, and ability to accomplish. Don't go to sleep worrying about what didn't get done, think about what you are going to do.

THE BOTTOM LINE

Relax. You are doing the best you can.

Taking Time For Yourself

Give yourself time during the week to recharge your batteries. This doesn't mean squeezing in an extra errand! Allow yourself a relaxed 'do as you please' time at least once a day.

In the early post-partum days this may be as simple as taking a warm soothing shower while someone you trust tends the baby. Later on it could be a half an hour at the library, a long walk without children, taking a class, writing a letter, anything - as long as you can identify it as something you're doing just for yourself.

THE BOTTOM LINE

You need your own piece of time for your own peace of mind.

Touching

Swap (or just plain get) massages from a friend or partner. Ten minutes is plenty, longer is great. Have your friend or partner focus on whatever part of your body seems to need attention; feet, forehead, shoulders, or wherever. Give yourself the freedom to ask for what it is that you need in the way of touching: slower, faster, softer, or firmer. You'll know what parts of you need the most strokes.

You can also use the self-massage places suggested in the "What To Do About It" sections in this book. The line of muscle attachments around the base of the skull (the nuchal line) suggested in the chapter on the neck is one such place (page 109). Five minutes of gentle work here will bring wonderful relief. Foot rubs (page 148) are also especially satisfying. They will energize you and leave you feeling less clogged up.

THE BOTTOM LINE

Your touch is one of your baby's fundamental emotional and physical supports - you deserve gentle touching from all those around you.

Eating Well

Give yourself the opportunity to eat slowly and thoughtfully. This is particularly hard if you have other children. Try to have at least one meal that's more than just gobbling the leftovers from the kid's plates.

Banish all thoughts of slimming diets. If you are nursing, you need at least 500 more calories a day over what you used to eat. In your early months post-partum the extra body fat is there for a purpose. Even if you're not nursing, you are recovering from nine months of steadily increasing work and the tremendous physical effort of birth. Don't worry about it; enjoy this time in your life.

Fluids are also important. They are twice as important if you are breastfeeding. Sometimes it's hard to remember to drink as much as you need. Have a glass of water every time you nurse your baby.

If there are foods or drugs that you gave up for the baby's sake, stay off them. This is true even if you choose not to nurse for very long. Your body will take several months or more to adjust to its new, unpregnant condition. Drugs and "sinful" foods will just confuse it.

Vegetarian mothers, particularly those who avoid all animal foods including eggs and cheese, need to be especially careful about getting enough calcium and vitamin B-12. The demands of nursing and pregnancy deplete both of these and we recommend that you consult with someone who is sympathetic to both breastfeeding and vegetarianism to work out a diet that's safe for you and your baby.

THE BOTTOM LINE

You're still eating for two.

Accepting Your Changing Self

As a new mother your body has undergone (and is still undergoing) profound changes. These will continue for some time. Understanding these changes and accepting and adapting to them will reduce your frustration.

Hormonal Changes

Most books tell you that the period of hormonal ups and downs lasts for three months after the birth. This is really an understatement. For most women it lasts for six months and for many it may be as long as a year. During this time, dramatic shifts in the levels of your estrogen, progesterone, and relaxin will affect the looseness of the ligaments around your joints, temperature regulation, feelings of hunger, water retention, and, of course, how you feel about everything.

It's very important to remember about the instability and looseness of your joints. You are going to be doing a lot of lifting and you need to protect yourself from injury. Be thoughtful and careful with yourself when you pick up your baby. In the early weeks after the birth always assume that your body is vulnerable and do things with care. The early chapters in this book will give you tips and techniques for doing simple things in sensible ways.

Organ Changes

As your uterus returns to its pre-pregnant size, you will probably experience gastrointestinal disturbances and alterations in bowel and bladder function. You may find that flatulence (gas) is almost as painful as labor and more common than you usually experience. This is especially true for women who have had a cesarean section. Everyone should read the chapter on the pelvic floor (p.13). Read it now, if you haven't already, and learn the Kegel exercises.

Metabolic Changes

Another major shift that is occurring involves your body's use of fats and glucose. During your pregnancy these substances were being metabolized, mobilized, and directed to the developing fetus, now they're being directed back to you. As your body shifts its goals, you will probably also experience differences in secretions such as sweat and mucus and in the amount of energy you feel. This is normal and your body will adjust.

Everything Is Changing!

Your hormones, your internal organs, and your metabolism are all changing, you've just gone through a major, nine-month long physical effort, and a new person has just entered your life - forever. Is it any wonder that your emotions are bouncing around?

Especially Your Feelings...

You may find yourself crying a lot, feeling out of touch with yourself, and unsure of what you want from life. This is disturbing, but not unusual. Post-partum depression is real. For most women it's not serious, it's just the sum total of all that you've been through - and it's a lot. Your body is different inside and out, your hormones are all over the place, and you're exhausted.

You will certainly experience golden moments. You will also experience some not-so-golden ones. They are normal and everyone has them. Don't let these moments make you feel bad or weird or different from anyone else. What you need most of all is support and a sympathetic ear. Talking with your partner, other mothers, counselors, friends, or family members can help. Most of all, be patient with yourself.

The changes that you are experiencing will settle down. The old saying, "the only constant is change," was never truer than now. Everything is different in your life, your family, your emotions, and your body.

THE BOTTOM LINE

**Life will return to normal - well, normal plus one.
Enjoy the changes and appreciate yourself.**

Appreciating Yourself

After the early weeks, you will find that the ooohs and ahhhs fade, your sleep is interrupted, diapers pile up, and the softly focused, golden moments slowly pass. Life, as the Beatles put it, goes on. You may experience turmoil at the thought of ever balancing working and mothering. You may be oppressed by the drudgery and confusion of staying home with the baby while ordinary life resumes. You may find that feelings of failure creep in. Suddenly you start to think...

"I'm not a good mother because _____."

        a) I'm going back to work.

        b) I'm not going back to work.

        c) I would do better with a boy.

        d) I would do better with a girl.

        e) I don't have enough energy.

        f) I'm an emotional wreck.

        g) All of the above

        h) A million other reasons.

Feeling this way is perfectly normal and sometimes hard to counteract. We live in a society that is long on sentimentality and short on practical support. "Oh, what a beautiful baby!" is not always followed by "and what about you, what can I do to help?" New parents often feel isolated and inadequate once the glow is off and the pressure is on.

The best cure for this (and any other feelings of inadequacy), is to appreciate yourself. Take time, right now, to celebrate your enormous accomplishment. You have grown, nourished, sheltered, and birthed a new human being with your body. Only you could have done this at this time, in this way, and for this child.

THE BOTTOM LINE

By the time your baby begins to use first words and take first steps, you will have spent almost two years doing an exhausting, frustrating, exhilarating, wonderful job.

Thank you!

The Working Parent
(extra effort needs extra care)

It Ain't Easy...

being a working parent. It's hard on bodies, minds, and souls. Most of all, it's physically hard.

Our bodies were designed for movement. Unfortunately (for our general well being), we no longer squat, jump, walk, run, stroll, roll, climb, or relax as much as our ancestors did. We tend to sit a lot, sometimes awkwardly. Our hands are cramped over keyboards, our necks crooked over telephones, and our shoulders hunched over steering wheels. What's worse, we remain in these positions for long periods of time.

The result is that a few of our muscles get overworked, cramped, and generally abused, while the rest lie unused. When our work is over, we rush home. At home we frantically try to squeeze a day's worth of domestic activity, lifting, hugging, feeding, and cleaning, into the few hours left between supper and sleep.

It doesn't sound like fun. It becomes a lot less fun when the mix of static daytime posture and frantic evening activity add up to muscle spasms and strained tendons. Everything still has to be done, but now through a haze of aches and pains.

Helping Your Body

Your body needs movement to function well. This doesn't mean you have to run six miles at your lunch break or keep a set of weights under your chair. It does mean you have to get yourself to do some kind of stretching or physical activity so you can break the routine of static posture. This will keep you limber and healthy.

There are always times when things seem just too busy for any kind of real break, but most of the time there will be opportunities to take care of your body, if you make it a priority. Even at your busiest, you can always squeeze in thirty seconds here and there to do something.

It can be as simple as standing up and looking around or shaking out your wrists. If you have a job that involves the same kind of movement over and over again, it means finding a stretch or alternating movement that will balance the overworked parts of your body.

Take Just A Moment For Yourself

- Try one of the short stretches from the body sections in this book. If your neck or upper back is tight, rest your hand at the base of your neck and breathe in so that you hand is lifted by your breath. This will only take seconds, but it will relax muscles right down to the center of your back and undo hours of bending forward at a keyboard. If your wrist bothers you, try bending your hand backward as if you were examining your fingernails. This will stretch tense forearm muscles and allow your wrist to move in a different direction.

- Imagine yourself doing a more pleasant activity. If you let yourself relax and then visualize yourself swimming, playing volleyball, or whatever, your body will remember, and those very different sets of muscles will get a tingle.

- Give yourself a little self massage on some particularly annoying spot.

- If you're waiting at a stop light, square your shoulders and let your chin drop down onto your chest for a second or two, then yawn.

- Take a moment, before you go to bed, to do a stretch or two. If you work at any occupation that requires you to hunch forward a lot during the day, the stretch can be just lying on your back on the floor and letting your shoulders sink back into the rug for a couple of minutes.

Helping Your Head

So much for your body, what about your head? Frenzied, rushed, harried, these are all words that can be used to describe large chunks of the working parent's time. The one thing that will make time work for you is organization.

Organization does require extra effort up front. But spending five minutes in the late evening preparing the diaper bag for day care, or mixing formula, or getting an older child's lunch ready, means five minutes of grace in the morning when you really can use it. Whatever you can do to plan ahead will lighten your load. It will also cut down on the times when, in total "OH-NO-I'M-GONNA-BE-LATE" panic, you grab up your child at just the wrong angle for your back and spend the rest of the day with an ache. Instead, use those five minutes for a long, luxurious hug.

Once you're organized, stick in a little time to day dream. If there is a place that you've visited, a pleasant memory, a snatch of song, or anything else that gives you that sigh of mental relaxation, tuck it away. When you get frazzled, go to it. It's the mind's equivalent of a long, deep breath.

Helping Your Heart

There is one more obstacle. For many, it's the biggest of all. In order to work, your children have to be cared for by someone other than you. This leads to one short and very heavy word, guilt. For which there is one short and very powerful remedy. Forgive yourself. You are doing the best you can.

The more we learn about the health of the human body, the more clear it becomes that how you feel has a close relationship to how well you are. Stress leads us to rush and overtire our bodies, stick unnecessary or unhealthy things into them, and just plain not take care of them. So the root cause of many of our physical complaints is often the general state of our feelings. It's easy to forget that our physical selves and our psychological selves are wrapped up in the same body.

If you are a working person in our hyped-up industrial society, you are pushing or being pushed to the limits of accomplishment. If you are a parent in our hyped-up adult-centered society, you are pushed over the limits of ordinary endurance. If you are trying to do both, for whatever reason, you can multiply everything by three.

As a working parent you deserve praise, support, and nurturing (not to mention a good night's sleep)! Since you are unlikely to get as much of these as you need, you may as well do it for yourself.

The first step is to recognize any feelings of anger or resentment you have toward yourself. The second step is to replace self blame with self care. Feelings of guilt only make you take it out on yourself, and you need and deserve better. A long time ago a wise Rabbi, Hillel, said it all, "If I am not for myself, who will be? If not now, when?"

POLITICAL SUGGESTION: Parents perform the most important work in any society. Without them there is no future. And yet America, which should be a world leader, does less to support parents and children than any other industrialized nation. We will remain this way until parents, and all people who love children, take strong action. Write a postcard or phone your political representatives today and let them know how you feel. Have your parents and your friends do the same!

Biofeedback

Biofeedback is information that lets you observe how your body behaves. When thinking about your pelvic floor anything that helps you to become aware of these muscles and their activity can be considered biofeedback.

Biofeedback comes in many forms. It can be as simple as watching your muscles in a mirror, or as high tech as a computer assisted electrical device. Many people need some help to become familiar with the muscles of the pelvic floor. Biofeedback devices will educate you, and help you exercise these vital muscles more effectively.

Different Ways to Get Feedback

1. Watch the muscles contract by observing them lift up in a mirror.
2. Feel the squeeze and release with your finger inserted in your vagina.
3. Observe the recorded pressure with a Perinometer.
4. Observe muscular activity with a surface emg (electro myographic) unit.
5. Insert and hold in small vaginal weights.
6. Ask your partner to feel the squeeze during sexual activity.

Vaginal Weights

These weights are small, usually tampon shaped weights that are inserted in a tampon carrier. They come in sets of five with increasing weights. When placed in the vagina, they are held in by contracting the muscles. They are an excellent way to train yourself to pull up and in with your pelvic floor muscles while performing activities or exercises that require you to bare down or push out.

OtherDevices That Can Help

If there isn't enough sensation in the pelvic floor muscles to tell you when and how they are working, you will need an external guide during the early stages of recovery. The two general types mentioned here can be rented for home use. Consult with your health care practitioner about which is best for you.

Surface EMG Units

These are battery operated devices that provide a visual read out of how well the muscles function. Some of them can store a computer record of your exercise sessions. This can be used by your health care practitioner to monitor your progress. The sensors that detect muscle activity can be placed over the muscles outside the body or inserted inside the vagina.

The Perineometer

Dr. Kegel's device to show and measure the pelvic floor muscles in action is called a perineometer.

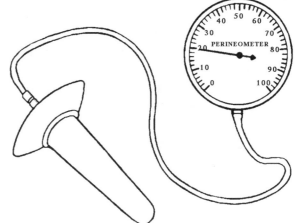

Your muscles compress a rubber probe inserted in the vagina. This forces air through a hose to a dial showing how much pressure the muscles exert. The harder the muscles contract, the higher the reading. Kegel's patients used this device for three twenty-minute sessions a day and had an 84% recovery rate from incontinence in seven to nine weeks.

Which To Choose?

The two kinds of bidofeedback device that sensitively record the activity of your pelvic floor are listed in the chart below. Either one can help you, but there are some differences that you and your health care provider should discuss so that you get the treatment best suited for you.

unit	Surface EMG	Perineometer
pluses	• external or internal sensors • can detect muscle relaxation • insertion not necessary	• treats specific muscles • softer • simpler to operate • easier to self monitor
minuses	• not always muscle specific	• doesn't really detect muscle relaxation
best for	• trauma of birth injury • need to monitor relaxation • when insertion not advised	• for specific muscle work • convenience

And MOST Important!

Learn and do the Kegel exercises. Remember to hold for 10 seconds each time for strengthening, relax the muscles, and throw in a few quick flicks. Try for 40 to 80 repetitions over the course of the day. This could be the best habit you ever acquire!

Tips

Do's

Remember that you are more vulnerable around the time of your period, and be extra careful when you lift and exercise.

Put up reminder notes. Leave a note over your changing table to remind yourself to lift carefully.

Wear comfortable shoes.

Don'ts and Do's

Don't step over your child gate—open it, then step through.

Don't always do things the same way—alternate sides for everything.

Don't lift and turn at the same time—lift first, then turn.

Don't hold your breath when you lift—exhale as you lift.

Love as You Lift

Talk to your baby while you lift. (When you talk, you exhale.)

Hug as you lift. (When you hug, you hold the weight close to your body.)

Take Stretch Breaks

Pause to stretch and relax frequently.

Never push yourself too far or too hard.

Use the basic exercises several times each day.

The Basic Exercises

Please Write to Us

HealthyWomen Resources is committed to publishing useful information for parents and children. We can't answer individual health inquiries or make medical referrals, but we would like to hear from you. Please write to us to comment on this book, suggest new ideas, or share resources and helpful information.

Bulk Rates

Special bulk rates are available, please write for details. (Individual price is $18 per copy plus $6 shipping and handling. MA residents add $0.90 sales tax)

Contact Us

HealthyWomen Resources
675 Massachusetts Ave. 10th floor
Cambridge, MA 02139

e-mail: HealthyPT@aol.com
Web: www.healthywomenresources. com

**HealthyWomen Resources, 675 Massachusetts Ave. 10 floor,
Cambridge, MA 02139**

☐ Please send me bulk purchase information.

☐ Please let me know about other HealthyWomen Resources publications.
I am particularly interested in: _____

☐ Please send me an additional (copy/copies) of

How to Raise Children Without Breaking Your Back

Name:_____

Address:_____

_____

_____

$18 per copy plus $6 shipping and handling. (MA add $0.90 sales tax)

Total Enclosed:$ _____